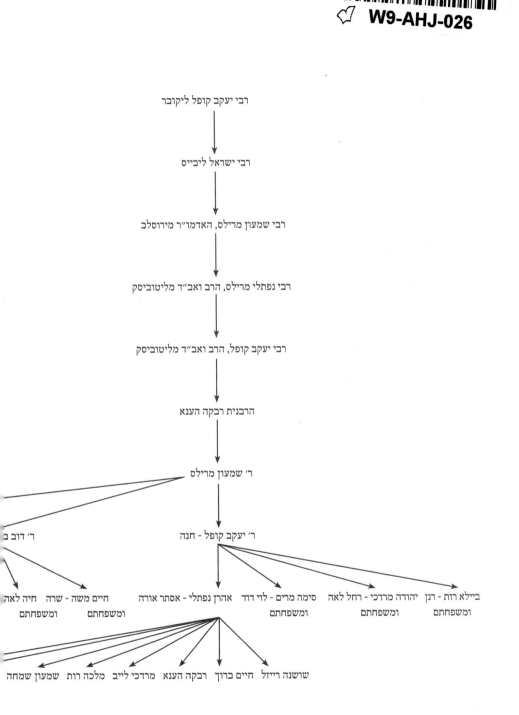

רבי יעקב קופל ליקובר

רבי ישראל ליביים

רבי שמעון מרילס, האדמו״ר מירוסלב

רבי נפתלי מרילס, הרב ואב״ד מליטוביסק

רבי יעקב קופל, הרב ואב״ד מליטוביסק

הרבנית רבקה העANא

ר׳ שמעון מרילס

ר׳ דוב ב

ר׳ יעקב קופל - חנה

חיה לאה   שרה - חיים משה   חיים משה - שרה   חיה לאה   אהרן נפתלי - אסתר אורה   לוי דוד - סימה מרים   רחל לאה - יהודה מרדכי   רנן   ביילא רות
ומשפחתם   ומשפחתם   ומשפחתם   ומשפחתם   ומשפחתם

שמעון שמחה   מלכה רות   מרדכי לייב   רבקה העANא   חיים ברוך   שושנה רייזל

Rebuilding the Foundations

CHICAGO CENTER
for
Torah & Chesed
Services for the entire community

UNDER THE LEADERSHIP OF
Rabbi Yehoshua Eichenstein
ZIDITCHOVER REBBE

Rabbi Pinchus Eichenstein
ROSH KOLLEL

Rabbi Tzvi Bider
EXECUTIVE DIRECTOR

Rabbi Daniel Muskat
DIRECTOR OF PROGRAMMING

Network of Programs:

TORAH
200 people learn daily

- KOLLEL KINYAN TORAH
- RUBEN SHAS KOLLEL
- KOLLEL DIRSHU
- MATEH ARON SRS. KOLLEL
- DAF DIGEST PUBLICATIONS
- COMMUNITY-WIDE
  FATHER-SON LEARNING PROGRAMS
- WEINSCHNEIDER TORAH SERIES
- YESHIVAS HAMASMIDIM
- SIMCHA DAVIS
  LEGAL HOLIDAY PROGRAM
- COMMUNITY-WIDE
  WOMEN'S SHIURIM
- TORAH TAPE LIBRARY

AVODAH
400 people daven daily

- CHESED L'AVROHOM
  COMMUNITY BAIS MEDRASH
- 16 DAILY MINYONIM

CHESED
Thousands benefit annually

- HACHNOSAS ORCHIM OF CHICAGO
- BIKUR CHOLIM FOR MEN
- REFOENU HEALTH CARE SOCIETY
- FOOD FOR SHABBOS PROGRAM
- HELPING HANDS
- TOMCHEI TORAH FUND
- MEDICAL ADVISORY SERVICE
- SENIOR WOMEN SOCIAL &
  LEARNING PROGRAM
- FREEBAY
- LEV CHASUNA
- GENETIC TESTING/
  HEPATITIS VACCINATIONS
- ACHEINU CALLING TREE
- CPR/ FIRST AID CLASSES
- ACHDUS BULLETIN
- TAXI AMBULANCE &
  PHARMACY SERVICE
- WELCOMING COMMITTEE
- ACHEINU SIMCHA GUIDE
- ADVANCED MEDICAL KITS
- RAPID STREP TESTING
- ACHEINU COMMUNITY DIRECTORY

This book is presented on the occasion of the Annual Banquet of the *Chicago Center for Torah & Chesed*. A biography of the dynasty of Yoruslav-Litovisk, it reaches back more than 200 years, to the era of the early Chassidic masters. It was in that era that the close relationship between the Eichenstein and Maryles families originated. The first Zidichever Rebbe, the *Aterez Tzvi*, Rebbi Tzvi Hirsch Eichenstein *zt'l*, and the first Yoruslaver Rebbe, the *Toras Shimon*, Rebbi Shimon Maryles *zt'l*, were both disciples of the Chozeh of Lublin. They forged a close friendship that has endured unto this day.

Rebbi Naftali Maryles *zt'l* of Litovisk, the son of the Yoruslaver Rebbe, was a *talmid muvhak* of Rebbi Eizekel (Yitzchak Isaac) *zt'l* of Zidichev. Rebbi Naftali's moving eulogy for his rebbi appears in his *sefer*, *Ayalah Shluchah*.

Reb Ari Maryles' grandfather, Reb Shimon Maryles *zt'l*, was the great-great-grandson and namesake of the Yoruslaver Rebbe. He learned and davened for many years in the shul that preceded the *Chicago Center for Torah & Chesed*. Reb Ari's father, Reb Yaakov Koppel Maryles, learns daily in the Mateh Aron Kollel.

With the founding and expansion of the *Chicago Center for Torah & Chesed*, Reb Ari has taken ever increasing responsibilities for its development. This year, Rabbi Ari and Esther Maryles have agreed to accept the *Community Service Award* at our Annual Banquet. To commemorate the event, they have published this biography of his grandfather and the Yoruslav-Litovisk dynasty. We trust that you will find it to be instructive and enlightening.

Rabbi Tzvi Bider
Executive Director
Chicago Center for Torah & Chesed

6350 NORTH TROY AVENUE, CHICAGO, ILLINOIS 60659 ● PHONE 773.761.4005 ● FAX 773.761.7603

REBUILDING THE FOUNDATIONS

The Dynasty of Yoruslav — Litovisk

Ari Maryles

TARGUM PRESS

Published by:
TARGUM PRESS, INC.
22700 W. Eleven Mile Rd.
Southfield, MI 48034
E-mail: targum@netvision.net.il
Fax: 888-298-9992
www.targum.com

Printing plates by Frank, Jerusalem
Printed in Israel by Chish

Approbation to *Sefer Toras Shimon*

(718) 436-1133

RABBI YAAKOV PERLOW
1569 - 47TH STREET
BROOKLYN, N.Y. 11219

יעקב פרלוב
ביהמ"ד עדת יעקב נאוואמינסק
ברוקלין, נ.י.

בס"ד ערב ר"ח אלול תשנ"ו

הגדול הנעלה ר' חיים שמעון ני' הנה הגיד הגיד שמועה טובה את הליכותי לאור
ע"י מעיות אאמו"ר אבקנל הרהנ"ת ר' שאגל אולשער בל"ען לעיונים
דבר האבע אמר"ו נתם להל על פי ולא דעם הרהנ"ת ר' לאל
לאחיתרן בשין, ונערשלהו נחלם כן והי אם האיל עאאאי ולבי
הגאוית אמיו אבא ריבה לאחדע דבם הימולים דיבם הועלים
והי, וכון וה.ו. הנמי ... כתם ואלית ולולת של הגעית לעין את לעלהי"ם
ואון לעדני ורלאא, והוני דם ... על הימלע דרדם האלכת ואל אוי אל

ועזר ק' פרלוב

Approbation to *Sefer Toras Shimon*

Rabbi Yehoshua H. Eichenstein
6342 N. Troy Street
Chicago, IL 60659
(312) 973-5161

יהושע העשיל אייכענשטיין
בהרה"צ מוהרר"א ז זצ"ל
מזידיטשוב ־ שיקאגו

"ילכו מחיל אל חיל, יראה אל אלקים בציון" (תהלים פ"ד ח').

ידידנו היקר המו"ל הרב ר' אהרן נפתלי מרילס הי"ו הגדיל ציון לעשות ציון לנפש חי' עבור זקינו הרה"צ מוהר"ר נפתלי זללה"ה אבדק"ק ליטאוויסק בעמ"ח הספה"ק אילה שלוחה, ולהדפיס ספרו בשפה המדוברת פה אמעריקא לאחר שכבר הדפיס לפני שנה הספה"ק תורת שמעון של זקינו הרה"ק חו"פ הרבי ר' שמעון מיערוסלב זי"ע ועי"ז הריהו הולך מחיל אל חיל לפאר זכרון אבותיו הקדושים נ"ע ולהפיץ מעינותם חוצה.

ואמנם יש עוד נקודה חשובה המרחפת על פני כל פעולותיו וראוי להרחיב מעט הדבור עלי' וזה על פי מה שהובא בספר יושר דברי אמת (בסוף אות לג) בנוגע להתקשרות האדם בשעת התפילה לאותם שהם למעלה ולמטה ממנו.

וז"ל ובאמת שמעתי מפה קדוש הרב האלקי מוה"ר יחיאל מיכל [מזלאטשוב] זל"ה שאמר קודם כל תפלה אני מקשר את עצמי עם כל ישראל הן עם גדולים ממני והן בקטנים ממני ותועלת התקשרות הגדולים ממני שעל ידם תתעלה מחשבותי ותועלת התקשרות בקטנים ממני שיעלו על ידי ע"כ שמעתי מפיו הקדוש עכ"ל.

אדיר חפצו של המו"ל דנן הוי בדרך הנ"ל לקשר עצמו עם אבותיו הקדושים להתעלות בעצמו עי"ז ועם זה גם לקשר בניו ובנותיו וכל הבאים אחריהם שיכירו הכרה ברורה וחזקה החוב הקדוש המוטל עליהם להתנהג בדרך התורה בהצטיינות.

טמון בתוך זה גם רצון לעורר חבריו וידידיו ג"כ, שהרי לכל אחד ואחד יש אבות ואמהות מדורות הקודמים הראוים לשמש לדוגמא ולהתעוררות לעבודת הבורא ית' ולזהירות במצות התורה, ועל ידי שיראו חביריו וידידיו איך כל כך תפארת בנים אבוחם יתעוררו גם הם להסתכל למעלה ולהתנהג ולהתנהג למטה בצד היותר רצוי בדרך התורה.

ויהא רעוא מן שמיא שחפץ ד' בידו יצליח שיתקיימו כל שאיפותיו הנעלות ושיגיע עי"ז לסיומא דקרא הנ"ל יראה אל אלקים בציון עם כל צאצאיו זרע ברך ד'.

יהושע העשיל אייכנשטיין

Contents

Introduction

It was merely a matter of listening to a basic teaching of our sages that prompted me to publish this book at this time. Our sages teach in Avos (1:14), "If not now, when?"

A few years ago, I started writing this biography as a preface for the Sefer, *Ayalah Shluchah*, a collection of the *divrei Torah* of Rebbi Naftali Maryles זצוק״ל, the Rebbe of Litovisk (Lutowiska), who was the son of Rebbi Shimon Maryles זצוק״ל, the Rebbe of Yoruslav (Jaroslaw). Between 1999 and 2001, I had the great merit of reprinting the Sefer, *Toras Shimon*, of Rebbi Shimon Maryles, as well as the English translation of both *Toras Shimon* and *Ayalah Shluchah*. As I began to compile the preface for the reprinting of the Hebrew *Ayalah Shluchah*, I realized that there is enough information available to comprise a book in its own right about these special and holy people.

Rebbi Shimon of Yoruslav, and his son, Rebbi Naftali of Litovisk, were my forebears, who left us with a rich spiritual legacy. This legacy, dating back three hundred years to the times of the Ba'al Shem Tov, was nearly completely destroyed in just six years by the decimation perpetuated by the evil nation of Germany and its accomplices.

My grandfather, Reb Shimon, named for his illustrious ancestor, and two of his sons survived the conflagration. With the help of Hashem, they were able to begin rebuilding a world that had been lost.

Every Holocaust survivor has a unique story. That story encompasses his or her experiences in pre-war Europe, during the war, and the years after the war. Many of the stories contain within them hundreds of years of Jewish history, as is the case with my family's story. While each one's story of suffering, faith, and survival has much to teach us, the members of the new generation, unfortunately most survivors' experiences are left undocumented.

Moreover, while some memories fade as time passes, other memories surface as the years go by. As I completed this book, another heartrending recollection was related to me by Mr. David Huss, my dear friend and barber, regarding one of my relatives. Aunt Devorah was my father's שיחיה first cousin. She was the daughter of my Zayde's brother, Naftali. Devorah was married at a young age to a *shochet* who lived in Horodenka (near Lvov). The young couple had one child and lived a peaceful, happy, spiritually-rich life, following in the ways of their holy ancestors — until the war. Devorah's husband was taken away and killed. Not long afterwards, Devorah and her baby were herded into the cargo area of a truck packed with other Jews and driven into the forest. The truck stopped at a large pit, and the German soldiers screamed at the Jews to disembark and to go into the pit. When everyone was in the pit, the Germans fired their guns at their victims. Devorah instinctively tried to shield her baby by clutching her close to her heart. As it turned out, however, the baby shield Devorah instead; a bullet entered the baby's head just before Devorah's heart. Devorah pretended that she was dead and stayed in the bloody pit, covered by corpses, until the carnage was complete and the Germans left. Late at night, Devorah climbed out of the pit and ran through the forest, finding shelter at the home of a gentile farmer. From there she went to the countryside, where she found a cave where other Jews were hiding (including the future wife of David Huss). Devorah survived the war and remarried. She and her husband moved to Australia to start a new life. Tragically, however, this was not to be; Devorah was hit by a truck and died.

It is our duty to learn about the lives of our forebears and to rebuild the world of Torah and *emunah* that was lost.

I have the most profound feeling of appreciation for the Ribono Shel Olam, for all of the kindness that He constantly showers upon me and my family and all of Klal Yisrael.

My deep gratitude goes to my dear parents, Reb Yaakov Koppel and Chana Maryles, שיחיו לאורך ימים טובים. No words can ever fully express the appreciation that a son has for his parents, for all that they have done for him and continue to do for him. I am especially grateful to my father and my mother for sharing parts of their life story and experiences with me. It took great courage and strength for them to allow the memories to surface to the fore again. May they be blessed with good health and have much *nachas* from their children, grandchildren, and great-grandchildren, who are, and will continue to be, inspired by their example, having gone through so much in their lives yet without losing their *emunah* and remaining steadfastly dedicated to Torah and Mitzvos.

My wife's parents have been special role models for us. My father-in-law, Reb Moshe Aharon Mauer, שיחיה, is distinguished in his capacity as a community activist, who serves as a foundation pillar for many of the most worthwhile endeavors in our hometown and beyond. My mother-in-law, Fegi

Mauer, שתחיה, has taught us, through her actions, the meaning of a *ba'al chessed.* May they both have good health and continue to receive much *nachas* from their family.

Rav Yehoshua Heshel Eichenstein and Rav Chaim Twersky have generously given me their precious time to teach me about my ancestors and their teachings. The Eichenstein and Maryles families have been close for 200 years, beginning from the close bond between the Rebbe of Yoruslav and the Rebbe of Zidichev. I pray that our families continue to share a close relationship for many generations.

I thank Rabbi Yisroel Shaw for all of the effort that he put forth into making this book worthy of publication, as well as for his work on all of the other books on which we have collaborated (both the English and Hebrew editions of *Toras Shimon* and *Ayalah Shluchah*). From editing, proofreading, and researching, to working directly with the publisher and coordinating the many details that go into the production of a book, Yisroel has been there for me. On a personal level, it is not easy to find a better and more loyal friend than Yisroel. His friendship has enabled me to fulfill the dictum, "Acquire for yourself a friend" (Avos 1:6), in the most outstanding way.

Just days before this book was to go to press, I received the sad news of the passing of Rabbi Moshe Dombey, the founder and director of Targum Press. While my relationship with him over the past five years could be called "only business," there was no such thing as "only business" with Rabbi Dombey, for everything he did was infused with *yir'as Shamayim, ahavas Yisrael,* and, above all else, *Kiddush Hashem.* I will always remember the example that he set, and I will remain grateful to him for enabling me to publish the Divrei Torah and history of my ancestors.

I am grateful to the staff of Targum Press for their outstanding work on behalf of this book and the other books of my forebears that they have published. It has been a pleasure working with them.

I also thank Rabbi Pnuel Peri for the professional touch that he has put into the narrative. I look forward to working together with him on further projects of disseminating the Torah and history of pre-war Europe.

Most of the historical information about Rebbi Shimon of Yoruslav in this book is based on the outstanding research of Rav Meir Wunder, as recorded in his biographical work, *Ohel Shimon*. Rav Wunder is the world's foremost expert on the history of the Jews of Galicia. His research in *Ohel Shimon*, and certainly in his phenomenal five-volume work, *Meorei Galicia — Encyclopedia of Galician Sages* (Jerusalem, 1978-1997), gives us a glimpse of a special world that no longer exists, but from which, thanks to Rav Wunder, we can now glean guidance and inspiration for our own lives. Rav Wunder has restored for us a link in our ancestral chain, and to learn about the great people from whom we descended is an essential part of our *avodas Hashem*. I have profound respect and gratitude for Rav Wunder, and I pray that he be blessed with continued health and strength to carry on the important work that he does on behalf of Klal Yisrael.

As this book was being prepared for publication, Rav Doniel Rokeach, the Rav and Av Beis Din of the Yoruslav Beis Midrash (in Monsey and Boro Park), informed me that the Yoruslaver Rebbe's family gravesite had been located — over sixty years after its desecration during the war. I am grateful to Rav Rokeach for giving my family the opportunity to sponsor the building of a new *ohel* over the grave. As the plaque there reads, my wife and I dedicated the *ohel* in memory of my grandfather, the great-great-grandson of the Yoruslaver Rebbe and his namesake. I am also thankful to Rav Rokeach for providing me with photographs of the gravesite, which have been included in this book.

Lastly, but most importantly, I thank my wife Esther for standing by my side at all times, for being such a wonderful and supportive wife, for being the greatest mother for our children, and for sharing life together with me. May we be blessed with much *simcha* and *nachas*, and merit to see the ultimate and final exultation of the Jewish people at the arrival of Mashiach, *bimherah beyamenu*.

Ari Maryles
Chicago, 5766

Aharon's Bunker

The bell rang once, piercing the silence of night.

People sat up in their tiered, plywood beds and stared frantically through the pitch blackness of the bunker. One of the young men climbed atop the stove, placed his ear to the chimney and listened intently.

"There are Germans here," he said. "Everyone remain absolutely quiet and still."

The surviving members of the Maryles family, Reb Shimon and his brother Reb Yoshe, and two of Reb Shimon's teenage sons, Yaakov Koppel and Berish, listened and waited and prayed in the underground refuge which could only rightly be called Aharon's bunker.

The beds upon which they and more than thirty other Jews now sat, terrified, the water cisterns embedded in the earth beneath the bunks, the stove and chimney, the toilet and air ducts were all products of the genius, skill, and courage of Reb Aharon Maryles, a learned and devout Chassidic Jew.

From the moment Aharon began hauling dirt out from beneath the Schwartz family home at 59 Boryslawska Street in Drohobycz, Poland, his vision of the ten-foot by thirty-foot bunker, which would eventually conceal up to forty-five Jews until the end of the war, took miraculous shape. He had spared nothing, conceiving of a five-foot buffer zone of earth between the house's kitchen floor and the top of the bunker, and another buffer zone of earth beyond its side wall, before the house's cellar, as a precaution lest the Germans conduct a search of the house and attempt to find the bunker. Aharon connected the bunker's lights and gas stove to public utility sources before the private meters of the house, eliminating the possibility of an abnormally large electrical and fuel drain arousing the municipality's suspicions.

Even the bell, hung within the chimney from the kitchen stove above, was his doing. It was their warning system arranged with the gentiles living upstairs, a Ukrainian husband and wife who had claimed the Schwartz's home with the ghettoization of Drohobycz's Jews, yet who had consented, for an enormous fee, to the bunker's construction. One ring for danger. Two rings for all clear.

How ironic, then, that Reb Aharon Maryles, their brother and uncle, was not now with them, not in the bunker nor in this world at all, yet perhaps no more ironic than the demise of any one of the innumerable Jews who were murdered in those years while laboring tirelessly to spare their brethren the very fate which they themselves would not escape.

Now, for many hours the Maryles men and the others listened breathlessly in blackness to every thud and scrape above their tiny tomb. They heard the dull clop of soldiers' boots upon the kitchen floor upstairs, the distant barking of orders, the sound of furniture being moved and violently overturned, the breaking of floorboards and, to their horror, the digging of shovels and pickaxes.

Then, the digging stopped, and the house seemed quite.

The bell rang twice.

My father, Reb Yaakov Koppel Maryles, was a boy in that bunker in which my Zayde, Reb Shimon, also survived. I am named after Reb Aharon, who saved them and many others from death. I knew my Zayde well and, of course, my father and I are very close. However, in a certain sense they all remain mysteries to me. I am awed by Reb Aharon's resources to defy the Germans and save Jews, ultimately at the cost of his own life. Also, I am astounded by my grandfather's, father's and uncles' survival, their will to reconstruct lives that had been so deeply torn and scarred, to cling to the Torah despite their personal suffering and then even to infuse the children of the next generations, like myself, with love of that Torah. How did they do all of this? Who were they? Who are they?

Like all great Jews, they were and are products of a bygone world of which only echoes remain. For them, in particular, those echoes emanate from a certain point in space and time, from Eastern Europe in the year 1734, when, on Lag Ba'Omer of that year, the Ba'al Shem Tov revealed himself and founded what we know as Chassidus.

A Bygone World

The Beginnings and Flourishing of Chassidus[1]

A pillar of the Ba'al Shem Tov's teachings was that every action and emotion, through purity of intent, could be employed in serving G-d. One may (and must) eat with the intention of deriving strength with which to serve G-d. One may work with the intention of supporting one's family whose members, thus sustained, will likewise serve G-d. One may even sing and dance at a wedding with the intention of increasing the joy of the *chassan* and *kallah*. The Ba'al Shem Tov taught that all of one's daily acts may become elevated in the service of G-d, a doctrine which was readily accepted by the masses of his time, the majority of whom were oppressed by the prevalent hatred of the gentiles towards them, and who were depressed by the sense of despair at the lack of any relief forthcoming.

Two of the factors which contributed to the despair of the Jewish masses were the Cossack uprising in Poland led by Bogdan Chmielnicki and the false messianic movement of Shabtai Tzvi.

---

1 Much of the information in this section was culled from the books, *Chassidic Masters* by Rabbi Aryeh Kaplan (Moznaim Publishers), and from *Triumph of Survival* by Rabbi Berel Wein (Mesorah Publications).

In 1648 and 1649 the Cossacks, under the leadership of Bogdan Chmielnicki, rebelled against their Polish landlords in the Ukraine and invaded Poland. Sweeping through the countryside, they massacred enormous numbers of the Jewish population in what historians have labeled the largest scale slaughter of Jews since the Roman conquest in 70 C.E. until Hitler. This tragic period, which destroyed much of the Eastern European Jewish infrastructure, is called after its Hebrew dates, *Tach v'Tat*. It would not be until 1655 that Poland would begin to revert back to normalcy, communities would be rebuilt and yeshivas reopened, but all with a great toll having been taken on its Jewish inhabitants.

In the wake of the violence, loss, and despair of *Tach v'Tat* came the hope and fervor of messianic redemption in the form of Shabtai Tzvi, who in 1665 dealt a second severe blow to the Jews. A brilliant young Jewish scholar from Turkey who was well-versed in Kabbalah, he proclaimed himself the Messiah and established an enormous following in Turkey, Greece, Italy, Albania, Egypt, Syria, and Israel. He also had Western European followers in such places as Amsterdam, Hamburg, Frankfort, and Altona. Many Polish and Russian Jews of Eastern Europe also became enthralled with him.

Eventually, the Sultan of Turkey arrested Shabtai Tzvi and presented him with the choice of martyrdom or conversion. The false messiah chose the latter, inflicting upon the Jewish world a crippling psychological wound for which the Ba'al Shem Tov, nearly 70 years later, would reveal the salve of Chassidus, revitalizing and fortifying Judaism for the next two and half centuries until today.

There was much initial opposition aimed at the Ba'al Shem Tov. Ironically, while he was trying to rescue the Jewish people from the depressive aftermath of Shabtai Tzvi, he was being accused of fostering yet another false messianic movement. History bears out, however, that the Ba'al Shem Tov's opponents, though many, were assuring that another movement like Shabtai Tzvi's did not threaten to uproot the faith of the Jewish people and, as such, were acting for the sake of Heaven.

Even the best-meant adversarial intentions, however, would not stifle the proliferation of the Ba'al Shem Tov's teachings. Heavily based upon Kabbalah, they were recorded by one of his students, Rebbi Yaakov Yosef of Pulna'ah, who came to be known as "the Toldos" for his book, *Toldos Yaakov Yosef*, which enabled his master's ideas to be studied worldwide.

Another conduit of Chassidus through the succeeding generations was in the form of a second uniquely gifted student. It is said that before the Ba'al Shem Tov died, his *talmidim* asked, "Master, how can you leave us?" The Ba'al Shem Tov enigmatically replied, "There is a bear in the forest." This was a reference to his student, Reb Dov Ber, who became known as the Maggid of Mezeritch. While Rebbi Yaakov Yosef spread his master's teachings through his writings, the Maggid focused his efforts upon organizing leaders who could embody and disseminate those teachings throughout the Jewish world.

Although he was a prominent scholar in his own right, Reb Dov Ber chose the role of Maggid over that of Rav in order to insure a thorough and well-grounded spread of the Ba'al Shem Tov's teachings. In Rebbi Yaakov Yosef, the author and formal authority, Chassidus had a Rav, a halachic base. In Reb Dov Ber, the Maggid, or "teller," the nascent movement had a public voice with which to deliver its ideological worldview and humanistic lessons. From the Ba'al Shem Tov's death in

1760, the Maggid lived just twelve additional years, yet he managed to lay the foundation of Chassidus throughout Europe.

It could be said that while the Ba'al Shem Tov unveiled the seed of Chassidus, the Toldos and the Maggid sowed that seed throughout Europe. However, Chassidus only truly began to blossom through the efforts of Reb Elimelech of Lizensk, the originator of the concept of the *pidyon*, a contribution offered to a Tzaddik and often accompanied by a *kvittel,* a written request. Known as the "Rebbe Reb Melech," Reb Elimelech succeeded the Maggid, his teacher, following the latter's death. His students, in turn, greatly spread and mainstreamed Chassidus throughout Poland and Hungry. Among those disciples were the Chozeh (Seer) of Lublin, Rebbi Shimon Maryles (the Rebbe of Yoruslav), the Kozhnitzer Maggid, Rebbi Avraham Yehoshua of Apt, Rebbi Mendel of Riminov, and Rebbi Moshe Leib of Sasov. By the year of Reb Elimelech's death in 1787, Chassidus was well-known and growing in popularity throughout Eastern Europe under the leadership of outstanding scholars.

The Chozeh of Lublin

The fortification and ultimate dominance of Chassidus throughout Poland and Galicia can be attributed to one of Reb Elimelech's closest students, Rebbi Yaakov Yitzchak Horowitz, the Chozeh (Seer) of Lublin, who became known as the "Chozeh" because of an enlarged eye which developed by shielding his eyes with a cloth for three years from the tender age of twelve so as not to glimpse anything improper, and because of his ability to "see" that which most others could not.

He came from a home of scholars and geniuses. His mother, Matil, was the daughter of Rav Yaakov Koppel of Likov (who was also the grandfather of Rebbi Shimon Maryles, the Yoruslaver Rebbe), and he would himself mature into a leader of distinction, dedicating his life to two essential causes. First, the Chozeh strove to mainstream Chassidus among a Polish Jewry beset with strong opposition to the Chassidic movement, against whose followers the rabbinic forces in Vilna placed four proscriptions, three of which were made during the Chozeh's lifetime. Second, he resisted the spread of secularization among Polish Jewry caused by the "enlightened world" which Napoleon wished to establish with his conquest of Poland.

The Chozeh's teachings were based largely upon the teachings of Reb Elimelech and, as such, were grounded more in the Talmud than in Kabbalah and were more palatable to the masses than the esoteric expositions intended for great scholars. Rebbi Shimon Maryles, the Yoruslaver Rebbe, one of the Chozeh's primary disciples, carried on this methodology of teaching. However, the Yoruslaver Rebbe's son, Rebbi Naftali Maryles (the Litovisker Rebbe), became a student of the Rebbe of Zidichev, adhering more purely to the Kabbalistic approach evident in the writings attributed to the Ba'al Shem Tov and the Maggid.

Like Reb Elimelech's establishment of the *pidyon*, a crowning achievement of the Chozeh was his deepening of the role of the Rebbe, the Tzaddik, as an advocate for the people in all matters both spiritual and mundane. By the time of his death in 1815, Chassidus was well-established throughout Eastern Europe, the role of the Rebbe was better defined, and whatever antagonism still met the Chassidic movement was passing.

Rav Yaakov Koppel Likover

One of the Chozeh's closest students and followers to perpetuate his ideas was his cousin, Rebbi Shimon Maryles of Yoruslav. Born in 1761, a few months after the death of the Ba'al Shem Tov, to Rav Yisroel Leibis and the grandson of the great *mekubal*, Rav Yaakov Koppel Likover, the son of Rav Klonimus, Rebbi Shimon came from a family of G-d-fearing and scholarly *misnagdim*.

Legend has it that the Ba'al Shem Tov wanted Reb Yaakov Koppel to join Chassidus. However, Reb Yaakov was strongly opposed to the movement. On one occasion, when he saw the Ba'al Shem Tov approaching the doorway to his house, he jumped out of a window and fled, to return only after the Ba'al Shem Tov had left. The Ba'al Shem Tov entered the house and found Reb Yaakov's daughter-in-law there, who was pregnant with a child at the time. The Ba'al Shem Tov gave her a blessing that her child would grow up to become a great leader and teacher of Chassidus. The child was born and the Ba'al Shem Tov's blessing came true — the child grew up to be the great Rebbe of Yoruslav, Rebbi Shimon.

Reb Yaakov Koppel was very secretive about his knowledge and righteousness. He owned an inn and a winery in Likov, near Trenigrad, Poland, and he employed many workers who essentially maintained the business while he spent his days learning and performing acts of *chessed*. Gradually, however, people began to realize the greatness he concealed, and his acts of kindness gained renown throughout the Jewish world. From even a place as far away as Amsterdam came a request from the Jewish community that he go there and become their leader, but he humbly refused.

Another legend illustrates Reb Yaakov's broadening fame and, again, the esteem in which the Ba'al Shem Tov held him. During a series of merciless blood libels against the Jews, the Ba'al Shem Tov took council with Reb Yaakov and insisted that he travel to Rome to speak in person with the Pope and that there he would succeed in nullifying the terrible decrees against the Jews. (The sources that record this incident indicate that Reb Yaakov met with one of the Pope's ministers, who was born in Poland in a village near Likov and whom Reb Yaakov had helped by giving food and pocket money to him in his youth. Other sources indicate that it was the Pope himself whom Reb Yaakov had helped. According to either version, it was natural that Reb Yaakov should be selected for the mission to speak with the Pope.)

Reb Yaakov Koppel had many children, but we know details of only four of them. One son was Reb Yisroel Leibis, to whom Reb Shimon was born. A son, Reb Shlomo, was the patriarch of the Elbaum-Ortner families. Another daughter was the mother of Chana who married Reb Alexander Sender of Zidichev, whose son was Rebbi Yitzchak Isaac Yehuda Yechiel Safrin of Komarno. Finally, a second daughter, Matil, married Rav Avraham Eliezer Horowitz, and was the mother of the Chozeh of Lublin.

Rav Avraham Eliezer died at the young age of 42. He learned for fifteen years after his marriage and then became the Rav of Josefow, Poland. Following his untimely passing, his son — who would become renowned as the Chozeh of Lublin — was raised by his grandfather. Although the Chozeh would become a Chassid and his grandfather, Reb Yaakov Koppel, was, as mentioned earlier, opposed to the Chassidic movement, they maintained the utmost respect for one another, their common bond and love being the learning of Torah. Indeed, in a dispute with Rebbi Baruch of Medzhibozh, the Chozeh once exclaimed: "How can you consider yourself greater than I? You may be the grandson of the Ba'al Shem Tov, but I am the grandson of Reb [Yaakov] Koppel of Likov, may his memory be blessed!"

Reb Yaakov Koppel passed away on the fifteenth day of Adar Rishon, 5529 (1769), and was buried in Trenigrad. He left his own Torah insights unpublished, although one of his *chidushim* on the vowelization of the name "Yehoshua Bin Nun" is cited in the work of one of his grandsons, *Heichal HaBrachah* (Parashas Beha'aloscha), in the name of the Chozeh. Other *divrei Torah* of his are recorded in the name of the Chozeh in other books (see *Ohel Shimon*, p. 7, fn. 20).

Following Reb Yaakov's death, his son, Reb Yisroel Leibis (who signed his name as "Yisroel Elbaum," and whose given name was "Yisroel Leib"), moved to Josefow with his brother-in-law, Reb Avraham Eliezer. Reb Yisroel was a close student of Reb Yehuda Leib Margolios, with whom he often held elaborate halachic discourses. Two of the many *she'elos*, halachic questions, scrutinized in those exchanges, together with Rav Margolios' responses, were published by Reb Yisroel in his book *She'elos u'Teshuvos Pri Tevu'ah*, a treatise which reveals its author's high degree of scholarship, exceptional scrupulousness in Mitzvah observance, profound fear of Heaven, and thorough concentration in and devotion to prayer.

Rebbi Shimon Maryles:
The Beginnings

Reb Yisroel Leibis had a son named Shimon who later would take the last name of Maryles (when the government decreed that all persons must choose a proper family name), an acronym derived from the name of his father, M'Rebbi Yisroel LeibiS, an act indicative of the respect which characterized their relationship despite their differences on issues of ideology.

When Reb Yisroel relocated to Josefow, he left Reb Shimon to be raised by his grandfather, Reb Yaakov Koppel, and during that period Reb Shimon became very close with his cousin, the Chozeh, who was a disciple of the Noam Elimelech, Rebbi Elimelech of Lizensk. Apparently, Reb Shimon had become a follower of Reb Elimelech by the time of his Bar Mitzvah.

Reb Yisroel, decidedly opposed to Chassidus, was not happy about his son's decision to become a Chassid, which occasioned debate between the two over various issues. For instance, Reb Yisroel could not understand why Chassidim did not cry while reciting the Tachanun supplication and, indeed, why they sometimes skipped it altogether, such as on

the *yahrtzeit* of a Tzaddik. Conversely, Reb Shimon was puz-
zled why those who were not Chassidim did not cry each
morning while reciting the words of *"Eizehu Mekoman."*
That Mishnah, recited as part of the morning prayers each
day, begins its teaching of the precise location and method of
the offerings in the Beis HaMikdash with the words *"eizehu
mekoman shel zevachim,"* — "Where is the place of the sacrifices?", a rhetorical question which opens the Mishnah's dis-
cussion and which Chassidim read and internalized
independently as: "Where, because of our sins, has the chosen
place for G-d's commanded sacrifices gone? The Beis
HaMikdash has been destroyed and all of the sacrifices have
been abolished! Alas, where is their place!" Reb Shimon could
not understand how *misnagdim*, those opposed to Chassidus,
could hold back their tears through *Eizehu Mekoman* each
day at the onset of the morning prayers, allowing themselves
to cry only upon reaching *"v'Hu Rachum"* ("And He is merci-
ful") which is said toward the end of the prayers, at the beginning of Tachanun and, at that, only twice a week, on Monday
and Thursday.

For his part, Reb Shimon explained to Reb Yisroel that
Chassidim have a special time to cry and pour out their
hearts, and that time is at midnight during *Tikun Chatzos.*
"Why then should one cry further when reciting Tachanun?"
he would ask.

It was known that Reb Shimon was very meticulous regarding the recitation of *Tikun Chatzos.* He was always awake
by *chatzos*, midnight. Rav Avraham Cohen, of blessed memory, one of the great sages of Yerushalayim of old, relates that
midnight never found Rebbi Shimon asleep. Once he sat with
his disciples until near midnight, and then went to sleep. Fifteen minutes later they saw he was awake and asked him to

explain what happened. He told them that when he was still a baby in a cradle his mother took him out of his bed each night at exactly midnight and put him on the cold floor so that he become conditioned to weeping at this time.

Prior to his death, Reb Yisroel Leibis instructed his son to recite the mourner's Kaddish for him without the words, *"veyatzmach purkanei vikarev meshichei"* ("and may He cause His salvation to sprout and bring near His anointed one"), a supplementary phrase recited in Kaddish according to the Chassidic custom. The two, father and son, traveled to Rebbi Yaakov Meshulam Orenstein, the *Yeshuos Yaakov,* for a judgement as to whether Reb Shimon should indeed honor his father's command, and the decision rendered was that the phrase should be omitted in accordance with the father's wish.

When Reb Yisroel passed away on the 16th of Nissan, 5572 (1811), Reb Shimon honored their agreement. In the Beis Medrash of his cousin and teacher, the Chozeh of Lublin, he recited Kaddish in accordance with his father's will, but he recited it quietly while standing near the stove at the far side of the study hall so that no one would hear the omission. One day, following the prayers, the Chozeh approached him and said, "Your father, my uncle Reb Yisroel, appeared to me and asked that I tell you that you may say the words, *'veyatzmach purkanei.'* In the upper world he has seen that the way of Chassidim is proper."

Reb Shimon recited this phrase in Kaddish for the remainder of the year of mourning, and yet, interestingly, he omitted it each successive year on his father's yahrtzeit in deference to his father's original wish. Such sensitivity was characteristic of the respect that had always distinguished their relationship. As mentioned earlier, each one had held the study of Torah to be life's primary and absolute focus. Such was the basis of their shared admiration and, too, of their differences. Reb Shimon understood that his father's objection to the inclusion of *"veyatzmach purkanei"* in Kaddish was not based upon emotional bias but upon Torah reasoning and interpretation, so it was his father's Torah that Reb Shimon continued to honor each year by reciting Kaddish with deference to his father's original wish and the ruling of the *Yeshuos Yaakov*, even in the face of Reb Yisroel's revelation from the upper world. We know, after all, that Torah is "not in the heavens" (Devarim 30:12); accordingly, what Reb Yisroel saw in heaven in no way compromised the integrity of his original position in this lower, earthly world, and Reb Shimon understood this well.

As seen in his regard for his father's opinion, Reb Shimon took the words and advice of Tzaddikim very seriously. He understood that there was great merit in heeding even their seemingly insignificant wishes. Reb Yisroel had another son, Moshe, who once visited the Rebbe, Rebbi Tzvi Hirsh of Riminov, and was asked by the Rebbe for eighteen *adumim*. Reb Moshe refused, and he later related the incident to his brother. Reb Shimon ordered him to purchase insurance for his business immediately. Reb Moshe did so on Friday. On Motzai Shabbos, his business was entirely destroyed in a fire, and the insurance covered all but eighteen *adumim* of the loss.

The Noam Elimelech

As mentioned earlier, Reb Shimon was very young when his father, Reb Yisroel Leibis, departed for Josefow. Beginning from that time, Reb Shimon became very close with his cousin, Rebbi Yaakov Yitzchak Horowitz, the Chozeh of Lublin, and became his disciple. The Chozeh himself had studied under the Noam Elimelech, the Rebbe Reb Elimelech of Lizensk, of whom Reb Shimon also became a follower. At the time of his Bar Mitzvah, he visited Reb Elimelech, and the Rebbe placed Tefillin upon Reb Shimon for the first time, saying, "Come and I shall place the Tefillin of the Master of the world upon you." It was a gesture of honor which left an indelible impression upon the boy. Reb Shimon later exclaimed that if they would give him a crown in Gan Eden, then he would pass it on to his Rebbe, Reb Elimelech, who in turn would pass it to Rebbi Dov Ber, the Maggid of Mezeritch, who would pass it to the Ba'al Shem Tov, until it would reach all the way to Mashiach, who would receive all of the crowns. Reb Shimon explained that the Gemara's use of the words *"atarosehem b'roshehem,"* "their crowns upon their heads" (Berachos 17a), refers to the crowns of Tzaddikim upon their single head, meaning their leader, the Mashiach, who is called the head and first of all of them (Pesachim 5a).

Reminiscing about his years in Lizensk with Reb Elimelech, Reb Shimon once told a guest on the night of Bedikas Chometz that in Lizensk they would hear the thunder and lightening of *Matan Torah*, the Giving of the Torah, every Shavuos, yet in Lublin they heard them only once.

Reb Elimelech is said to have saved the town of Yoruslav from a plague that had afflicted the children. The town's rabbinic leadership sent a letter to Reb Elimelech asking him for a solution. Reb Elimelech responded that although he was neither "a prophet nor the son of a prophet," he would suggest that they monitor their *shochtim*, the ritual slaughterers. The town promptly engaged a Torah scholar to inspect the halachic integrity of its *shochtim*, who were overheard soon thereafter saying that they must now be careful to cease doing what they had been doing as they were now being monitored. The town investigated and corrected the matter, and the plague ceased.

Apart from miraculous insight and salvation, Reb Shimon witnessed exceptional holiness within the seeming mundane, commonplace environment of Reb Elimelech's life. Once, while visiting his Rebbe for Shabbos, Reb Shimon noted to one of Reb Elimelech's sons, Reb Elazar, how the servants were helping and contritely trying to appease one another as though it were the eve of Yom Kippur. Reb Shimon attributed their actions to the intense holiness of Reb Elimelech's Shabbos and its natural effect upon all present, even the servants.

Reb Shimon followed the Noam Elimelech as his primary Rebbe until his cousin, Rebbi Yaakov Yitzchak Horowitz, accepted the mantle of "Admor" and Reb Shimon became dedicated to him. This shift would become a sensitive matter as Reb Shimon would seek to maintain his new allegiance without slighting the honor of his former Rebbe. On one occasion, the Chozeh had a baby boy and wanted the Noam Elimelech to be the *sandek*, so he sent Reb Shimon to personally inform the Rebbe, Reb Elimelech. Reb Shimon was faced with a dilemma. When delivering the message, he did not want to slight Reb Elimelech's honor by referring to the Chozeh directly as his Rebbe, but to simply say that "Reb Yaakov Yitzchak" had sent him would be an unforgivable slight to the Chozeh, besides the fact that it is forbidden to call one's Rebbe by his untitled name alone. He and the Chozeh together assembled a solution. "My teacher and Rebbe, who sets me on the right path," Reb Shimon told Reb Elimelech upon seeing him, referring to the Chozeh, "invites the Rebbe of all of Israel to be *sandek.*"

Reb Shimon's concern for the honor of others did not extend inward, toward apprehension over his own honor. This is most clearly evident in his practice of frequently traveling to Tzaddikim who were much younger than he, even in his old age. Also, in following the Chozeh, Reb Shimon had accepted as his Rebbe a first cousin, an act of exceptional humility which few others would have been able to do. Reb Shimon, however, simply felt that the Chozeh could be his best teacher, and that was his sole concern.

One of the many teachings which the Noam Elimelech imparted to Reb Shimon was the importance of eating the fourth Shabbos meal, the Melaveh Malkah, at the departure of Shabbos. Reb Elimelech, himself, did not conduct a public Melaveh Malkah, and it is said that he was thus never visited by Dovid ha'Melech, who was not pleased about this practice.

Once, however, Dovid did come to Reb Elimelech, disguised as a fish merchant bringing fish for the Melaveh

Malkah meal. Reb Elimelech told him that he no longer had the strength to begin conducting a public Melaveh Malkah each week but that he would instruct his descendants and his followers to be especially careful to observe this Mitzvah.

Once, Reb Elimelech's son, Reb Elazar, was visiting the Maggid of Kozhnitz, and during the Melaveh Malkah some men entered and asked them to pray for a woman who was having great difficulty in childbirth at that moment. The Maggid, however, did not dispatch Reb Elazar to the Mikvah for immersion and then to the Beis Medrash or some holy site to pray for the endangered woman. They simply sat and continued with the Melaveh Malkah. When they had reached the hymn of "Eliyahu Ha'navi," news arrived that the woman was well and had given birth to a baby boy. The Maggid then revealed in the name of his father that anything one desires during the meal of Melaveh Malkah can come to fruition during that time. Also, Reb Elimelech once said that "a great *segulah* for women to have an easy childbirth is eating after the departure of every Shabbos a special food for the sake of Melaveh Malkah." Therefore, both his disciples and his descendants, including Rebbi Shimon of Yoruslav, made it their practice to conduct a public Melaveh Malkah following every Shabbos.

Rebbi Shimon's mentor, the Chozeh of Lublin, was also very careful to observe the meal of Melaveh Malkah. He said that the Mitzvah of Melaveh Malkah is so important that the author of the Shulchan Aruch gave it its own chapter (Orach Chaim 300), even though that chapter contains only one line, in order to emphasize its importance.

It was Rebbi Shimon's practice to eat milk or milk fat at the third Shabbos meal (because milk is symbolic of mercy).

Rebbi Shimon conducted his Melaveh Malkah publicly, as he was a disciple of Rebbi Elimelech and the Chozeh of

Lublin. He also did it because he was a man who excelled in the attribute of kindness and mercy to others, even to others who did not deserve it. Accordingly, he was concerned that the wicked people who were being punished in Gehinnom, but who received a reprieve every Shabbos, would not be sent back to Gehinnom so quickly once Shabbos departed. Therefore, he delayed the time of his Melaveh Malkah meal as much as possible in order to delay the return of the wicked people to Gehinnom. He delayed the time of his Melaveh Malkah meal until Sunday morning, when he would sit with his followers and conduct a public Melaveh Malkah. They would pray the morning service and then sit down in their Shabbos clothing, and the meal would last until the afternoon hours. It is because of that practice that, for many generations, it was the custom of all of the synagogues in the town of Yoruslav — even the ones that did not follow Chassidic customs — not to recite Tachanun on Sundays.

The source for Rebbi Shimon's practice of delaying the Melaveh Malkah meal is an incident related in the name of Rebbi Moshe Sofer of Pshevorsk. Rebbi Shimon was visited one Motzai Shabbos by the souls of two deceased individuals who asked him to do them a favor. Upon inquiring as to how they were being treated in the next world, he was told by one of them that due to not having conscientiously observed Melaveh Malkah during his lifetime, he was forced to return every Motzai Shabbos to the hardships of Gehinnom. The other soul, who had been very careful about eating Melaveh Malkah, replied that his reentry into Gehinnom was forestalled as long as there was still a Jew in the world who had not yet partaken of Melaveh Malkah. This is why the holy Rebbi Shimon delayed his Melaveh Malkah to Sunday morning.

At his Melaveh Malkah, Rebbi Shimon sang the song, "Ish

Chassid," with a holy beauty, which the Tzaddikim highly praised. On one occasion, when Rebbi Shimon spent Shabbos in Belz, the Belzer Rebbe, the holy Rebbi Shalom (the "Sar Shalom"), greatly desired to hear the song when sung by Rebbi Shimon, and so he asked his followers to summon him before Rebbi Shimon began to sing. When Rebbi Shimon began to sing "Ish Chassid," Rebbi Shalom stood just outside the door, and signaled to his followers not to let Rebbi Shimon know that he was there. At that time, Rebbi Shimon was very old and had already lost his eyesight. However, he immediately sensed the presence of a great person and he tapped with his finger and said, "My young Rebbi is here!" and he refused to sing. Rebbi Shalom implored him to sing and not to disturb himself from his holy service, but Rebbi Shimon refused, saying that he was unable to sing while his Rebbi was present. Only after the Belzer Rebbe left did Rebbi Shimon continue his holy service.

On another occasion, the two of them sat together at a Melaveh Malkah meal. Rebbi Shimon asked, "Why did Eliyahu Ha'navi have to do things that were beyond the normal course of action in order to bring wealth to that 'Ish Chassid' (the 'righteous man' whom the song 'Ish Chassid' discusses), such as sell himself as a slave, build a building through the night, and so on (when he could have simply done a miracle instead)?"

Rebbi Shalom answered, "When Eliyahu Ha'navi is sent to carry out a certain mission, he is granted the ability to do anything. But when he is not sent, he is not able to do any more than you and I."

Rebbi Shimon's explanations for the songs sung at the Melaveh Malkah on Motzai Shabbos are included with the rest of his divrei Torah in Toras Shimon.

Ordination

Rebbi Shimon continued to be very close with Reb Elimelech until the Rebbe's death in 1787, even though prior to that time Reb Shimon had, as mentioned, accepted Rebbi Yaakov Yitzchak Horowitz, the Chozeh of Lublin, as his primary Rebbe. The two were very close even in Reb Shimon's youth, and when the Chozeh moved to Lublin, Reb Shimon would visit him frequently despite the hardships of the lengthy journey.

Students of the Chozeh would meet in Yoruslav and then travel from there to Lublin, often on foot as they lacked the money to rent a wagon. Once, as the group set out on its journey, one of its members, Rebbi Naftali of Rupshitz, suggested, somewhat lightheartedly, that Reb Shimon reveal himself as a Rebbe and then people would give them money so that they could hire a wagon. Reb Naftali further insisted that he would be Reb Shimon's personal attendant throughout the trip. Reb Shimon, of course, refused, and the group headed on foot toward Lublin.

At one of the inns in which the men lodged, Reb Shimon blessed the innkeeper, who was childless, that a son would be born to him. The man protested, saying that his wife was not only barren but already too old for childbearing. Reb Shimon assured him that his blessing applied nonetheless, and, in order to appease the innkeeper, he wrote an amulet for his wife containing the letters, "CKSPDMM," an acronym for the Polish phrase, *"Chociaż krowa stary, przecież dzieci może mieć"* which means, "Even though the cow is aged, she can still have children."

By the time of their arrival in Lublin, the Chozeh had already perceived with his "seeing" eye all that had transpired on the journey and declared to Reb Shimon, "Shalom Aleichem unto you, the *Rebbe* Reb Shimon! You are already dispensing blessings and writing amulets!" It was understood that the Chozeh thereby officially ordained Reb Shimon as a Rebbe.

Ordination, of course, did not diminish the undying love and unquestioning respect which Reb Shimon had for his Rebbe. Whenever Reb Shimon visited Lublin, the Chozeh would show him exactly where to sit in his Beis Medrash and, invariably, would direct him to the same seat. In the floorboards in front of this chair, a nail protruded which would pierce the flesh of Reb Shimon's foot, opening a deep wound from which he would not heal until well after his return to Yoruslav. Visit after visit, Reb Shimon would be directed to the same chair and suffer the same wound, yet he was never deterred from traveling to Lublin nor was he ever inclined to question the Chozeh.

Needless to stay, consistent with his character, Reb Shimon kept his ordeal with the nail in the Chozeh's Beis Medrash to himself, most likely because he never considered it an ordeal but, rather, one of life's many necessary challenges, especially considering that it was orchestrated through his Rebbe. The story would never have come to light had Rebbi Yissachar Dov, the Belzer Rebbe, not somehow become privy to it. When some of Reb Shimon's Chassidim sought to leave his Beis Medrash for a larger place of study, the Belzer Rebbe insisted that the Chassidim remain with Reb Shimon, relating this story to illustrate Reb Shimon's greatness.

Reb Shimon's desire for spiritual growth beneath the shadow of his Rebbe superceded even the accepted protocol for such growth. Most Chassidim utilized a visit to their Rebbe as an opportunity for *teshuvah*, repentance, and, as such, would stand at their Rebbe's right side, a gesture accepted by the Rebbe as an indication of his Chassid's current inner penitential struggle. Reb Shimon, however, could not devote himself to *teshuvah* while in the presence of the Chozeh, for so deeply positive was the Rebbe's influence upon him that he desired only for the Rebbe to see him fully, regardless of his flaws. It was with that internal, spiritual exposure that he stood at the Rebbe's right side. The Chozeh told Reb Shimon that while his intent was admirable, one should perform *teshuvah* whenever possible and that it was worthwhile concentrating on repentance, even if only for a moment.

The Trait of Joy

Given the intensely positive nature of Reb Shimon's relationship with the Chozeh, it is not surprising that Reb Shimon's trait of happiness for which he was renowned was learned from the Chozeh. It is interesting to note that the Chozeh was not naturally a *ba'al simcha*. In his youth with the Rebbe of Nickelsburg, the Chozeh had completely separated himself from all worldly pleasures, a spiritual achievement of distinction, to be sure, but one which, if prolonged without *simcha*, could have disastrous long-term effects upon the soul.

In reference to the young Yaakov Yitzchak Horowitz, the Rebbe of Nickelsburg therefore pleaded to the Rebbe Reb Zusha to "save the spirit of our Itzikel, please!" Reb Zusha taught the Chozeh to remain above worldly pleasures yet with true joy, and the Chozeh, a dedicated student, soon intertwined his essence with *simcha*. So thoroughly did he advance in this area that the Munkatcher Rebbe, Reb Shapiro, said of the Chozeh that "each of the great Tzaddikim in his day had a special trait, and that of the Chozeh was *simcha*." As in everything else, Reb Shimon received this trait from his Rebbe completely and unreservedly.

The Trait of Humility

As discussed, Reb Shimon's life was enriched not only with joy but also with unbounded humility and selflessness. This trait, too, he received from the Chozeh. While he had already possessed it to some great degree in order to accept a first cousin as his Rebbe, he refined it as a Chassid of the Chozeh. The Chozeh instructed Reb Shimon to visit as many Tzaddikim as he possibly could, declaring that "if you want to live a long life, subordinate yourself before every righteous person." He took this to heart, as he did everything the Chozeh taught him, and within his lifetime of 90 years he visited over 250 Tzaddikim.

One of Reb Shimon's travels was to Rebbi Yisroel of Ruzhin, the first Ruzhiner Rebbe. When he entered the room, the Ruzhiner stood up and declared, "Your face is shining with sparks of light from the countenance of Rebbi Shimon bar Yochai!" Reb Shimon explained that the Chozeh had blessed him that he should be "as strong as Shimon, the son of Yaakov, and as righteous as Rebbi Shimon bar Yochai, although a little less righteous is also good."

The Ruzhiner Rebbe would refer to Reb Shimon as, "Shimon the Righteous from the remnants of the Men of the Great Assembly." Reb Shimon would comment that while it was a mistake to call him "Shimon the Righteous," it was proper to say that he was from the remnants of the Men of the Great Assembly, meaning the assembly of men who had merited to know the Noam Elimelech.

That some of the special men to whom Reb Shimon journeyed were much younger than he was entirely inconsequential to Reb Shimon, even as he neared the end of his life and was quite advanced in age. In this conduct one may see how his traits of *simcha* and humility were actually intertwined. Although the world and his followers knew him as a Tzaddik, Reb Shimon did not consider himself with such regard, and thus he humbly cherished the opportunity to visit and learn from men who had reached great spiritual heights. Once with them, he rejoiced in their accomplishments and, most likely, reveled all the more if they were much younger than he and had managed to achieve so much in relatively so short a time.

A number of incidents demonstrate further Reb Shimon's trait of humility. The Rebbe of Sanz, Rebbi Chaim Halberstam, and Rebbi Shimon of Yoruslav were once attending a wedding. Just as Reb Shimon was about to wash before eating bread, Reb Chaim grabbed the washing cup and refused to hand it over until Reb Shimon had promised to write a note to Reb Chaim's *mechutan* beseeching him to end a bitter dispute that had developed between him and a certain person. Some of those present were very upset with Reb Chaim's apparent act of disrespect to Reb Shimon, but as they began to protest, Reb Shimon insisted that his honor was unimportant and that Reb Chaim deserved, in fact, praise for placing Hashem's honor and peace between Jews as his priority, even at the risk of social indiscretion.

Reb Shimon nurtured a special reverence for Rebbi Yaakov Reinman of Narel. When he would travel to Narel, he would dismiss his attendants at the city's outskirts, claiming that he no longer needed them because the light of Torah shining from within the town would serve as his guide. It might have seemed odd to the Jews of Narel to see the Rebbe of Yoruslav arriving in their town unattended, and, indeed, it would have been strange had it been conceived as some attention-getting gesture. Matters of perception and impression, however, never even occurred to Reb Shimon, for, in his view, would not anyone seeing the light of Torah approach it naturally and unaided?

When Rebbi Yaakov Reinman died, Reb Shimon continued visiting his son, Reb Avraham, whose daughter married Reb Nachum, the son of Rebbi Asher Yeshaya of Rupshitz. At the time of one of Reb Shimon's visits to Reb Avraham, the sons of the Rupshitzer Rebbe were present and sat immersed in Kabbalah. When Reb Shimon entered the room, the sons moved to the side and continued quietly amongst themselves, not wishing to alienate him, for they mistakenly believed that he was not well versed in the hidden parts of Torah. Reb Shimon approached them and said, "It is written, 'For You have exalted Your word even beyond Your Name' (Tehilim 138:2). This means that reciting Tehilim is even greater than being immersed in Hashem's hidden Names."

Why, though, did Rebbi Shimon Maryles of Yoruslav, beloved grandson of the famed Kabbalist Rabbi Yaakov Koppel Likover, not respond to their assumption of his ignorance with a demonstration of his talents, which indeed were awesome? Why did he address them only with an ideological stance on the importance of the recitation of Tehilim, which seemingly was an affirmation of their assumption? In truth, there is no explanation for his choice of words other than that he simply believed them. Beyond that truth, he had no considerations. Here, again, Reb Shimon's humility, so thorough as to seemingly board on innocence, reared itself without regard for impression and perception. His was a humility beyond humility, for to be humble for humility's sake is one thing, while to be so naturally, even unconsciously, humble as a result of adherence to truth is quite another. Complete and selfless alliance with truth is the essence of humility.

It is worth nothing that the importance that Reb Shimon placed on the recitation of Tehilim has remained prevalent in the Maryles family from the time of Reb Shimon. From my earliest years, I recall my grandmother saying Tehilim unceasingly. In endeavoring to remain faithful to my roots, I try to complete the full Sefer Tehilim each month. In the merit of Reb Shimon and those who came after him, may our family continue in his footsteps throughout the generations.

As Rebbe and Rav of Yoruslav

The Chozeh loved Reb Shimon and gave him a book of *Selichos* from which only he had prayed. Reb Shimon cherished this gift, and it has remained through the generations within the family, being presently in the possession of Rabbi Naftali Maryles of Boro Park, New York. (It is worth nothing that Rebbi Shimon's Kiddush cup is now in the estate of Rav Tuvia Halberstam, of blessed memory, in Boro Park.)

The two remained very close until the Chozeh's passing in 5575 (1815). Even before the Chozeh's death, Reb Shimon had become known as a Tzaddik and Rebbe in his own right, yet he humbly preferred concealment within the shadow of his Rebbe. After his Rebbe's passing, though, he could no longer obscure himself, and he would soon be forced into his rightful station as a leader and advocate for the Jewish people.

Reb Shimon lived in Yoruslav even prior to the Chozeh's death, although it is not known for certain why he chose it as home. His wife, Baila, was from there, so presumably Reb Shimon lived in Yoruslav so that she could be near her family. It may also be that he was drawn to live there because of Rebbi Zecharya Mendel, who was the Rav of Yoruslav during the years 5514-5555 (1754-1795) and one of the closest disciples of the Noam Elimelech. He also authored the book *Darchei*

Tzeddek and was famous for supporting Rabbi Yonason Eibshitz in his dispute with Rabbi Yaakov Emden. It is most probable, however, that Reb Shimon was attracted to the general spiritual atmosphere of Yoruslav's Jewish community, which was filled with Torah scholars and exceptionally devout people. Indeed, Chassidim used to call the town *"Yiras Lev,"* altering its proper pronunciation to express the "fear" of heaven in the "hearts" of its Jews.

The rabbinic leaders of the city appointed Reb Shimon as Rav of Yoruslav. Among these were Rabbi Yehuda Heller Vallershtein, Rabbi Naftali Hertz Charif, Rabbi Yaakov Yitzchak Horowitz, and the premier *dayan* of the city, Rabbi Leibush Horowitz. Reb Shimon was very active within the community thus entrusted to him, particularly with the establishment of proper *mikvaos* and the maintenance of a high standard of *shechitah*.

When the city decided to build a large synagogue, Reb Shimon became deeply involved with the project, even though its success would surely result in a siphoning of Jews from his own small Beis Medrash. Nothing more than this bespoke the purity of his love for Torah, the spreading of which was his sole concern regardless of who accomplished its proliferation.

Additionally, Reb Shimon headed a special committee which helped raise funds for poor families which could not afford to pay gentile youth to take the place of their children in fulfilling the mandatory Austrian military service (Galicia, from 1772 until 1918, was part of the Austrio-Hungarian Empire).

Despite Reb Shimon's prominence in Yoruslav, the Maskilim became a force in the region during Reb Shimon's lifetime, and he battled them incessantly. It was related in the eulogies following Reb Shimon's death that he had fought the Maskilim until they were "unable to lift their heads." He did so, however, not violently, but through prayer. Reb Shimon's ways were of peace and forthrightness, rather than of storms and upheavals, so for all of his powerful, albeit quiet, offensives against the Maskilim, they never focused their campaign directly against him.

The inhabitants of Yoruslav loved Reb Shimon, and he loved them. He used to jokingly say that "in far away places, they don't know me so well, so they err in calling me 'The Great Rav, Rebbe Shimon of Yoruslav'; in my region, however, they know me a little better, so I am called 'The Rav, Rebbe Shimon of Yoruslav'; in my city they know me even better, and I am called 'Reb Shimon'; but in my home, my wife knows me the best and simply calls me Shimon."

Not only did unadorned friendship and genuine admiration characterize Reb Shimon's relationship with his fellow Jews of Yoruslav but, also, with the many Chassidim who lived far from Yoruslav and who would travel to see their Rebbe and remain with him, sometimes for a few months at a time, before returning home recharged and revitalized with Torah and Chassidus. Reb Shimon opened his home to these people and cared for their needs, and his *hachnasas orchim* became legendary.

Reb Shimon cared for people's spiritual needs as well and gained renown as one who could effect personal *yeshuos*, salvations. Although this intensified the flow of guests from all over Galicia and Hungry to his home, he treasured the opportunity to receive and help more and more people. Characteristically, he did so graciously and naturally, without the slightest interest in building a following or broadening his Chassidic court. Many of his visitors were often surprised by his perfect command of the Polish language, which he exhibited unabashedly when it was difficult for someone to communicate with him in Yiddish. Although, in his circles, the usage and mastery of the gentile tongue was looked upon with disfavor, he cherished communicating with and reaching out to people through whichever medium was at his disposal.

Reb Shimon's fame increased further with the passing of the Noam Elimelech. Many of the followers of the Noam Elimelech unofficially accepted Reb Shimon as their Rebbe. Reb Shimon shared many of the same qualities of his former Rebbe, the foremost among them being a love of both Tzaddikim and simple, common Jews. The Noam Elimelech, in fact, told his brother, Reb Zusha, that this love is what supplied him, personally, with the power to bring about *yeshuos*.

Reb Shimon's love for common people and Tzaddikim alike accompanied his awesome humility. He was very close with a certain Tzaddik, the saintly Rebbi Yehuda Tzvi of Strettin. Once, Reb Shimon and Reb Yehuda Tzvi were traveling in separate carriages and they passed one another on the road. The drivers immediately halted on their command as each one leaped from his carriage to be the first to greet the other. Standing in the road, the two great men realized each other's intent, and Reb Shimon declared that he now understood the words of the sages that "two men can meet, but not two mountains."

In the same spirit, Reb Shimon commented that the Gemara (Berachos 64a) states that *talmidei chachamim*, Torah scholars, bring peace to the world. Why, he asked, are scholars referred to as *talmidei chachamim*, which literally means "students of scholars?" Should they not simply be called *chachamim*?

The Gemara is teaching us, Reb Shimon continued, that when one thinks of himself as only a "student of the sages," regardless of his actual erudition, he is capable of lowering himself before other great people and he increases peace in the world. If, however, he considers himself a great scholar in his own right, then he will not humble himself before great people and there will be no peace. Reb Shimon then explained the similarity of the incident in meeting Rebbi Yehuda Tzvi in the street to the saying that "two men can meet, but not two mountains." Two people, who both believe that they are the greatest, will not go out to greet one another, yet if they remember that they are only lowly men, then each person will dispense with his own honor and run out to greet his friend.

On a different occasion, another Tzaddik, Rebbi Moshe Leib of Sasov, once came to Yoruslav, and Reb Shimon ran to greet him, saying, "Shalom Aleichem, my Rebbe and my teacher!"

"Leave this 'Rebbe' title and come with me!" Reb Moshe Leib replied sharply. He led Reb Shimon to the market where he purchased two large bundles of straw. The two men, each shouldering a bundle, walked for a long distance until they reached a dismal, broken down hovel on the outskirts of town. Inside, they found an impoverished new mother. Reb Moshe and Reb Shimon spread the straw on the cold earth floor, cared for the woman and her child and then left.

It was a simple task, albeit burdensome, for which they easily could have dispatched some of their Chassidim, none of whom would have allowed the Rebbes to haul bundles of straw had they seen the great men emerge from the market. In their own eyes, however, they were not so great, and they viewed a Mitzvah which had come into their hands as an opportunity which they never would have traded for pomp and ceremony. Like men, rather than mountains, they met, and like eager youngsters, rather than esteemed elders, they ran to do their Mitzvah.

Happy With His Lot

Although his life was dedicated to the needs of people, Reb Shimon shunned the public's financial support. He and his wife, therefore, opened up a small leather goods store from which they could earn a meager living.

One of their regular customers was a priest from a neighboring village who would purchase leather goods for the people of his community. It once happened that Reb Shimon's wife was unable to be present in the store when the priest was due to arrive, and she told her husband to take special care of him, as he was their biggest customer. When the priest later entered the store, Reb Shimon was engrossed in reciting Tehilim and motioned for the priest to go and buy from one of his competitors. Giving up money was easy for Reb Shimon, but disappointing his rebbetzin was far less so. However, curtailing his *avodas Hashem*, his service of G-d, for money, even for a moment, was simply an impossibility.

Managing the store necessitated that Reb Shimon endure the hardship of traveling to far off places in order to purchase merchandise, sometimes even as far as Budapest. Moreover, even with the store's income, he and his family were extremely poor, and it was not uncommon for their household to feel the pangs of hunger. Reb Shimon, nonetheless, accepted his lot fully and with total trust in Hashem. He was not tormented in the slightest by the fact that his grandfather, Rabbi Yaakov Koppel Likover, had been very wealthy. Nor, for that matter, did the material wealth of the Chozeh, his cousin and Rebbe, becloud the way in which he viewed his own poverty. The Chozeh was known to bless people that they should become wealthy and grow closer to G-d through their wealth, yet that did not give Reb Shimon cause to begrudge his own impoverishment, but, rather, to strive for closeness to Hashem precisely through it.

Reb Shimon's poverty, like any hardship, provided an opportunity to grow and develop in his *avodas Hashem*. Poverty enabled him to perfect his trait of *bitachon*, trust in Hashem.

Reb Shimon was very close with Rebbi Meir of Frimishlan and once sent regards to Reb Meir through a local merchant traveling from Yoruslav to Frimishlan. Upon his arrival, the merchant greeted Reb Meir with regards from Reb Shimon and, as it was customary for Rebbes to send one another gifts, Reb Meir entrusted the merchant with five gold coins and many *grushes* for Reb Shimon on his return to Yoruslav. When Reb Shimon eventually received the gift, his rebbetzin, who was ignorant of the exchange between the two men, informed him that her pantry was empty and needed restocking. Reb Shimon asked her how much she needed, and the amount that she told him was the exact amount of Reb Meir's gift.

For Reb Shimon, the experience most likely was more than a remarkable display of Hashem's *hashgacha*, His careful, direct involvement in our lives. It was a lesson in poverty and, simultaneously, a Divine confirmation of the closeness to Hashem which he had achieved through poverty. Hashem was teaching him that, indeed, poverty was his lot, that the luxury of savings and of surplus was not to be his, for no sooner had the money reached Reb Shimon's hand than it was, in its entirety, taken away for bare necessities. Within that lesson was Hashem's unmistakable approbation of Reb Shimon's spiritual attainments, of the incalculable spiritual wealth which he had amassed in his life and which had made him worthy of such clear Divine revelation.

Ruach Hakodesh

Reb Shimon was, in fact, no stranger to Divine revelation and was known to exhibit powers of *ruach hakodesh*. There was once a very wealthy man in Yoruslav who chastised Reb Shimon for his impoverishment and seeming inactive life.

"Chassid! What do you do?" the man once demanded of Reb Shimon.

"I serve Hashem," Reb Shimon replied.

"And where does Hashem live?" the man scornfully asked.

"When you have to come up with bread for supper," Reb Shimon said, "you will know where Hashem lives."

Not long after that exchange, the man lost all of his wealth and became destitute, begging in the streets for scraps of bread.

Rebbi Yitzchak Elazar Shapira of Lancut and his son, Reb Shlomo (who later became the Rav of Strizov and Munkatch), traveled together a number of times to Reb Shimon. Reb Shlomo once testified that Reb Shimon not only saved him during a life-threatening childhood illness but also beseeched Hashem to add fifty years to his life. Before his death, he related that "my entire presence in this world has been through a miracle. When I was a lad of only twelve, I became deathly ill, and the doctors feared for my life. On the eve of Sukkos, my holy father saw my terrible, deteriorating state, and he sent a gentile (rather than a Jew because of the impending arrival of Yom Tov) with some *pidyon nefesh* money and a note, telling him to deliver them with great speed to the holy Tzaddik, Rebbi Shimon in Yoruslav. My father then went to pray. Before he had even finished praying, he was called to return home and stand by his dying son, may Hashem have mercy, for I had lost consciousness and slipped into a coma.

"I remained as such for a number of hours, and then, suddenly, I awoke and sat up in bed. I requested a little milk to drink, and from that moment on I began to recover. When the gentile returned from Yoruslav, they asked him what time it was when he was with the Rebbe, and it emerged that he had been with the Rebbe at the exact moment that my soul returned to me and I awoke. He produced a letter written by the *gabbai* which related that although Reb Shimon was quite advanced in years and, as was well known, had become blind, he received my father's note and *pidyon nefesh* money and knowingly said, 'If he is now still in this world, he will remain alive.' His prayer worked and provided me with an entire jubilee of years."

When Reb Shlomo Shapira was in need of salvation for his own unborn child, Reb Shimon was again forthcoming. Reb Shlomo's rebbetzin had suffered a miscarriage and faced with trepidation the prospect of carrying another child to term. She went to Reb Shimon and he blessed her, saying that the child she was then carrying would be born healthy and would mature into a *talmid chacham*. The boy whom she later bore was Reb Tzvi Hirsh, the author of *Darchei Teshuvah*.

Reb Shimon used to make yearly visits to the town of Lubice, near Warsaw, to rest. Each morning he would have the town's boys, of ages of seven to nine, brought to him for the recitation of the morning blessings. Once, the young Shmuel Abba of Zichlin was brought to him, and although the boy was then only six years old, Reb Shimon saw in him great potential and requested that the boy be brought to him with the older boys each day. At the end of his stay, Reb Shimon called Shmuel Abba into his special room and told him that he would give him a special gift — the gift of the ability to tell time to the exact minute by looking at his Tzitzis. This was revealed years later, when some of Reb Shmuel's Chassidim tried to trick him into remaining in the town of Lodz over Shabbos despite the Rebbe's express wishes to spend Shabbos elsewhere. On Friday afternoon, they furtively turned the clocks back a few hours, hoping that the Rebbe would unwittingly stay until it was apparently too close to sundown to travel. However, Reb Shmuel gazed down at his Tzitzis, announced the exact time to his shocked Chassidim, and related his boyhood story of Rebbi Shimon of Yoruslav's gift to him.

Strength and Longevity

Reb Shimon was nearly as well-known for his physical strength as he was for his spiritual prowess. It was said in Yoruslav that when he would bang his fists upon the table with exceptional force, the table would split. Interestingly, it is related that he could crack open a walnut by pressing it against the side of his neck (an act with apparent Kabbalistic significance).

Once, two robbers invaded Reb Shimon's home on Friday night while he was reciting Tehilim. Much to the robbers' astonishment, Reb Shimon subdued them, tied them up, and resumed his recitation! When he finished, he untied them and let them flee.

It is also related how Reb Shimon personally saved Rebbi Moshe of Pshinsk, the primary teacher of the Chozeh, from freezing to death. Reb Moshe lived in isolation and affliction, and one winter he nearly died from the cold of his bare shack in the woods. Reb Shimon found him, carried him in his arms a great distance to his own home and nurtured Reb Moshe back to health.

Reb Shimon's strength lasted well into his old age. At nearly seventy, a set of twins — a boy (who would become the Rebbe of Litovisk, Rebbi Naftali Maryles, my great, great,

great grandfather) and a girl — was born to him. Reb Shimon used to pray that he have strength in his old age because he believed that *arichas yamim*, "length of days," was fruitful only if one had the physical wherewithal to continue serving Hashem.

As mentioned earlier, the Chozeh instructed Reb Shimon to visit as many Tzaddikim as he possibly could, declaring that "if you want to live a long life, subordinate yourself before every righteous person." However, Reb Shimon himself gave a different explanation for his longevity. From his youth, he accustomed himself to accept whatever tribulations come upon him with love. Even though his life was full of hardship, suffering, and poverty, he always accepted the justice of Hashem and said, "If, G-d forbid, I challenge Hashem, asking, 'Why do I deserve such suffering,' then in heaven they will answer me, 'Come here and it will all be explained to you!' Therefore, I preferred not to ask any questions so that they would not summon me to the next world to receive explanations."

This short but sharp insight breathed encouragement and strength into those who dwelled in the shadows of hell, in the darkness of the concentration camps during the Nazi regime. Rabbi Tzvi Hirsch Meisels, in his book *Mekadshei Hashem* (Chicago, 5715/1955, pp. 15-16; see also *Ohel Shimon*, footnote 11), relates that when he arrived at Auschwitz, he endeavored to protect the silver lining (Atarah) of the Tallis of the *Yitav Lev*, the Satmar Rebbe, an heirloom in his possession. After much effort he found it among the confiscated items, and he cut the Tallis to the size of a Tallis Katan and wore it as an undergarment. Nevertheless, the kapo, a German Communist, saw that his clothing was bulging, and the kapo interrogated him. When Reb Tzvi Hirsch answered, "*Es ist ein Gotteskleid*" ("it is a G-dly garment"), the kapo pounded him with beatings and ordered him into his office, where, he said, he would like the Jew to teach him something about G-d. Upon entering the room, the kapo beat Reb Tzvi Hirsch with more blows and commanded him to stand up and explain how it is possible for a person to believe that Hashem exists when he sees the evil that is happening all around him. Reb Tzvi Hirsch answered him in succinct words, explaining that mere mortals cannot understand the ways of Hashem's conduct, just as a sick person does not understand the treatments that the doctor does for his benefit, and only in the end will it be understood. Reb Tzvi Hirsch then related to the kapo the insight of Reb Shimon, which is recorded in his father's book, *Binyan Dovid*. His words were pleasing to the gentile, who released him with no further abuse. Moreover, the kapo later called him to his block to receive extra portions of food, and in that way, with the help of Hashem, the life of Reb Tzvi Hirsch was saved.

Appreciation

Like longevity and stamina, the rudiments of life which all too often are taken for granted or even misused were constantly highlighted by Reb Shimon as things to be cherished. He therefore stressed the importance of one's wife and how, through her, one's children as well as oneself could be elevated.

Once, when he was advanced in years and already blind, Reb Shimon visited the Tzaddik, Rebbi Chaim of Kosov. In his host's home he was served a bowl of soup. After tasting it, he asked who had cooked it and was told that the rebbetzin had prepared the soup. Reb Shimon then commented that it had the taste of Gan Eden and, moreover, that when Mashiach would come he would seek out the rebbetzin to cook for him.

Those present were intrigued as to the inspiration for such high praise, and after investigating the matter, it was discovered that as the rebbetzin cooked, she prayed that her food nourish her husband and enable him to properly serve Hashem. Reb Shimon had tasted those prayers. He later told Rebbi Chaim of Kosov that the greatness of Rebbi Chaim of Kosov was of no great surprise, given that he had so righteous a wife.

Rebbi Yaakov Koppel Maryles *zt'l*, the Rebbe of Litovisk, the grandfather of Reb Shimon Maryles and grandson of Rebbi Shimon of Yoruslav.

The Rebbe of Sadigur, Rebbi Mordechai Shalom Yosef Friedman *zt"l*, whom Reb Shimon Maryles followed.

The present Rebbe of Sadigur, Rebbi Avraham Yaakov Friedman *shlita*.

The Chortkover Rebbe, Rebbi Yisroel Friedman *zt'l*, whom Reb Shimon Maryles followed before the war.

Reb Shimon Maryles, *zt"l*

Reb Shimon Maryles, *zt"l,* and his family.

A certification of appreciation presented to Reb Shimon Maryles by the Rizhiner Yeshiva.

תעודת הוקרה

לידידנו הנכבד והנעלה

הרה"ח ר' **שמעון מרילס** שליט"א

אשר זכה זקף על עצמו לכלכל מדי שנה
את ההוצאה הכללית של החזקת הישיבה

יום אחד בשנה

ושמו נרשם לזכרון עולם בתואר

פרס הישיבה

זכרה להם אלקי לטובה

זכות החזקת התורה זכות מרן קרוש ישראל מריזין זצוק"ל
יגן עליהם וימלא ה' כל משאלו' לבם לטוב להם כל הימים

בברכת התורה

הרב יהושע העשיל בריס
ראש הישיבה

הרב יוסף רבידביץ
מראשי מועצת הישיבה

JERUSALEM, 40 44 MALKEI ISRAEL ST. • TEL. 534700 .טל P.O.B. 5173 .ת.ד , • 44 40 מלכי ישראל רח' ,ירושלים

ארך ימים בימינה בשמאלה עשר וכבוד

A certification of appreciation presented to Reb Shimon Maryles by the Rizhiner
Yeshiva.

Yoruslav. The Great Synagogue, built in 1811, on Opolskiej Street. It was restored in 1990. (Photo courtesy of Jaroslaw Town Hall.)

Yoruslav. The city today, with the impressive Ratusz (City Hall) building, built in the mid-1800's. From the main town square, four main streets branched out, one leading to Radymno, one to Krakow, one towards the San River, and one was the center of the Jewish residents.

Drohobycz. The Jewish hospital, 1910.

Drohobycz. The Jewish orphanage, 1930.

Boz'nica= Synagoge.

Pozdrowienie z Droholycza.
Gruss aus Drohobycz.

Drohobycz. The synagogue as it appeared in 1900.

Drohobycz. A resident of Drohobycz during the war, with armband. (Photo courtesy of Yad Vashem.)

Drohobycz. A district synagogue, 1910.

Drohobycz. The "New Synagogue" on Orlynka Street. Construction began in 1842 and was completed in 1865.

Drohobycz. The "New Synagogue" on Orlynka Street. Construction began in 1842 and was completed in 1865.

Drohobycz. A view of the city today. (Photo courtesy of JewishGen <http://www.shtetlinks.jewishgen.org/Drohobycz/>.)

The newly-constructed *ohel* over the Yoruslaver Rebbe's gravesite. (Photos courtesy of Rav Doniel Rokeach.)

The graves inside the *ohel*.

The author, Ari Maryles, at the gravesite of his grandfather, Reb Shimon, in Jerusalem.

פ"נ

ר' שמעון מרילם ז"ל

בה"ר חיים נח שפירא ז"ל

נפטר בשיבה טובה וכשם טוב
ביום י"א אדר ב' תשנ"ב

"רבי שמעון אומר
שלושה כתרים הן
כתר תורה וכתר כהונה
וכתר מלכות
וכתר שם טוב עולה על גביהן"
אבות פרק ד' משנה י"ז

ת נ צ ב "ה

לזכר נשמות קדושי השואה
בײלא בת משה
יהודה בן שמעון
נח בן שמעון

The grave of Reb Shimon Maryles *zt"l.* Har HaMenuchos, *gush* 8, *chelkah* 2.

Talmidim

T he Yoruslaver Rebbe's teachings and ways influenced many of his generation's top students and future leaders. His primary student was Rebbi Shlomo Zalman (Yosef) Frankel, the Av Beis Din of Wialipoli (whose great, great grandson, Rav Shlomo Frankel, is the son-in-law of the present Zidichever Rebbe, Rav Yehoshua Heshel Eichenstein, who lives in Chicago and with whom I am privileged to share a close friendship). Reb Shlomo Zalman was Reb Shimon's entrusted attendant, who was ordained by Reb Shimon in the follow manner.

Reb Shimon, already quite aged and blind, was once waiting atop a horse-drawn wagon, and Reb Shlomo Zalman ascended the wagon's steps and stood beside the seated Reb Shimon. Sensing his presence, Reb Shimon asked, "Shlomo Zalman, is that you?" Reb Shlomo Zalman answered in the affirmative.

"You should know that I was ordained by the Rebbe, Reb Elimelech," Reb Shimon said, placing both of his hands upon Reb Shlomo Zalman's head. "And Reb Elimelech was ordained by Reb Dov Ber, and he was ordained by the Ba'al Shem Tov. The Ba'al Shem Tov was ordained by Eliyahu Ha'navi, so through the placing of my hands upon your head you are hereby ordained by Eliyahu Ha'navi. Go down from here quickly, for your state of holiness has risen, and it is no longer appropriate that you serve me."

Reb Shlomo Zalman soon afterwards became the Rebbe of thousands and gained renown as a great miracle worker who was capable of, among other things, discerning a person's personal acts by reading his handwriting.

Rebbi Yitzchak Isaac of Zidichev often visited Reb Shimon, whom he held in the highest esteem. Reb Shimon once asked Reb Yitzchak Isaac why the Rebbe bothered visiting him, and he responded that by visiting Reb Shimon one merited the blessing of, "Your world you shall see in your lifetime" (Berachos 17a). Reb Shimon's regard for Reb Yitzchak Isaac was mutually exalted. Reb Shimon's son, Reb Naftali, testifies in his book *Ayalah Shluchah*, "I heard from the mouth of my holy father, of blessed memory, when he spoke to the people who would gather beneath the shelter of his shade from the regions of Zidichev and Balachov, that they should seek out Torah from the holy Rebbe, Reb Dovid Zlatis of Balachov and the holy Admor, Rebbi Yitzchak Isaac of Zidichev, for they have true humility." Reb Naftali added that "many times Reb Yitzchak Isaac said to me that he wanted to do favors for me, especially in the merit of my holy father."

Rebbi Yitzchak Isaac Yehuda Yechiel of Komarno is counted among the disciples of Reb Shimon and sites many of Reb Shimon's *divrei Torah* in his books.

Rebbi Dovid of Dinov (Dynow) traveled frequently to Reb Shimon, and his father, the *Bnei Yissachar*, gave him a goblet cast from silver coins that had once belonged to Reb Shimon. The cup was enormous, holding a liter and one quarter of fluid, yet Reb Dovid used it together with a very strong wine for the four cups of the Pesach Seder and managed to remain awake the whole night and to recite *Shir Ha'shirim* with great devotion.

Rebbi Meshulam Feivush, the son of Reb Naftali Hertz of Barazan, often traveled to Reb Shimon. He resembled Reb Shimon in his ability to turn people to good through prayer rather than rebuke. Reb Meshulam's son, Reb Avraham Zerach Yehuda Leib, quotes Reb Shimon three times in his book, *Imrei Yehuda*.

Rav Yosef of Tarnopol, author of *Minchas Chinuch*, became close to Reb Shimon, visiting him twice.

Rav Yitzchak Isaac Weiss, the Av Beis Din of Swaliwa and Munkatch, also frequently traveled to Reb Shimon. The two met while in Belz.

A very close student of Reb Shimon, and even a possible successor to him, was Rebbi Eliezer Lipman Knavil, who was extremely precocious and virtuous even in his youth. Recognizing his greatness, Reb Shimon sought to bring him into his closest circle of *talmidim* and even to permit him to "see his face," referring to those aspects of Reb Shimon's *avodas Hashem* that were kept absolutely hidden. However, Reb Eliezer was not then certain that the path of Chassidus was the path for him, so he rejected Reb Shimon's offers.

A few years later, Reb Eliezer fell mortally ill, and the doctors were unable to cure him. His parents went to Reb Shimon to ask for a blessing that their son recover. Reb Shimon guaranteed them that Reb Eliezer would recover fully only if he accepted upon himself the ways of Chassidus. Reb Eliezer reluctantly relented. He spent twenty-two years under the guidance of Reb Shimon, until the latter's death. Even though Reb Shimon asked him to take his place after his passing, Reb Eliezer refused in the end to succeed his master out of humility.

Traveling to the Tzaddik

The act of "traveling" to a Tzaddik was not taken lightly. It was the quintessential expression of love, reverence, and honor for a Tzaddik in an era when travel occasioned many hardships and dangers now unknown to us. Equally unknown to us from that era, however, is the intensity of that love, reverence, and honor which drew great men to other great men regardless of the hardships. While we have, of course, Tzaddikim, they are largely peripheral to our daily lives, while for previous generations the righteous man was the teacher, confidant, and aid to whom Jews continuously and unreservedly turned.

So central to Jewish life was traveling to the Tzaddik that the "journey" was undertaken even when actual travel was impossible, as seen in the following teaching from Reb Shimon's son, Rebbi Naftali Maryles of Litovisk, published in *Ayalah Shluchah* (commentary to Shemos 25:1-2):

"I have heard it said of Chassidim and upstanding men of action, people who readily traveled to the Tzaddikim, to the righteous men of their generation, that when they were unable, for whatever reason, to travel immediately to the Tzaddik for aid in some suffering that had befallen them, they would separate from their money a charitable 'offering' and receive, thereby, salvation. I have heard from Rebbi Menachem Mendel of Radim that he, too, often traveled to my father's home in Yoruslav. On one occasion Reb Menachem Mendel, who had been caring for an ailing person, went to visit my father, but he was not home. Reb Mendel apportioned an 'offering' from his money, and the ailing person completely recovered. This phenomenon parallels what has been written in the name of the Ba'al Shem Tov, that the place to which a man's thoughts cling is the place where he actually and wholly is. Here, through focusing their thoughts on the righteous act of separating an 'offering' from their money, they themselves were with the righteous."

The Conduct of a Tzaddik[2]

Rebbi Shimon said that in his Shemoneh Esreh, he never added a single letter, but he followed the tradition that he had received from his holy teacher, the Chozeh of Lublin.

His prayers were said with melody and with softness, and not loudly or with shouting. Rebbi Shimon was quoted as saying that anyone who is able to assist the Chazan when he sings a melody during the prayers and refrains from helping is considered as though he transgressed the verse, "Do not stand idly by the blood of your fellow man" (Vayikra 19:16).

He said that before he prayed, he would not sell his Tefillah for all of the money in the world, but after he prayed he would sell it just to have a drink. (Perhaps he meant that he highly valued the act of Tefillah, which was more precious to him than anything, while he did not care about the reward for the act once it was done. In addition, perhaps he used so much of his energy for prayer that when he finished, he was so exhausted that he needed a drink to revive him.)

Rebbi Shimon maintained that machine-made garments for Tzitzis were valid, and as such he gave his endorsement to such a factory in Yoruslav. Whereas some authorities did not validate machine-made Tzitzis, Rebbi Shimon maintained

---

2   This section appears in the end of the English translation of *Toras Shimon*.

that one must not be excessively pious. Indeed, a woman once came to him with her baby and asked that he give the baby a blessing that the child grow up to be "good and pious." Rebbi Shimon answered, "Good — yes, he should be very good; pious — just a little."

Every Thursday, Rebbi Shimon would don an apron to bake Challah in honor of Shabbos. He would check to make sure that they were well baked. It once happened that the Rebbe of Belz saw him checking the Challah and he said that it was as if he saw the Kohen Gadol performing the service inside the Holy of Holies.

At the beginning of Kabbalas Shabbos, Rebbi Shimon would recite loudly the word, *"Lechu"* ("Go!") and then continue, *"Neranenah la'Hashem"* ("Let us sing praise to Hashem"), as described in *Toras Shimon* (to Tehilim 95:1).

On Friday night, when he would have to recite Kiddush between the hours of six and seven (Chassidim try not to recite Kiddush during that time), he would recite the prayer, "Av Ha'rachamim" (usually recited when the Torah scroll is taken out to be read in the synagogue), because it contains the words, "and He will save us from the bad times" ("the bad times" referring to the hours of six and seven).

Rebbi Shimon would pray early on Shabbos and Yom Tov. Once, when he finished praying on Rosh Hashanah and sat down to eat, he sensed that in the distant city of Belz, they were just beginning to blow the Shofar. He said in Yiddish, "The Rebbe of Belz is blowing into my soup."

Even though he had a very tender physical make-up, it was his practice to immerse himself in a cold Mikvah without concern. However, he instructed others who were weak not to go to the Mikvah, but that it sufficed if they washed their hands. His son related that Rebbi Shimon said, "Do not go to a Mikvah if you are weak, but instead wash your hands in the customary manner (which suffices as if one immersed in a Mikvah), as is written in the name of the Tzaddik, Rav Matali of Chernobyl. And if you do not believe [that washing one's hands is considered like immersing in a Mikvah], then you have not gone out of harboring heresy" (this is because the Gemara in Berachos (15a) derives from a verse that washing one's hands before prayer is akin to immersion in a Mikvah, and one who does not accept that is considered as though he rejects the words of the Gemara).

He was lenient with regard to drinking a hot drink before praying each morning. It is related that a certain prominent rabbinical judge from Hungary (who was not Chassidic) once spent a Shabbos in Rebbi Shimon's home. When Rebbi Shimon offered him a cup of hot tea before the prayers, the rabbi refused. When Rebbi Shimon asked him about it, the rabbi said, "To drink something hot before the prayers is not necessary to add life to one's spirit." Rebbi Shimon responded, "You have spoken wisely, for indeed, it is not necessary to add life to one's spirit, for without a hot drink before the prayers, one's spirit has no life!"

Regarding the use of liquor for Kiddush during the day on Shabbos (regarding which there is considerable debate about the amount one must drink), Rebbi Shimon said, "Either one makes Kiddush like a goy, or one drinks like a goy!" (That is, by being lenient and using the smaller amount, one's Kiddush is lacking, but if one is stringent and uses the larger amount, then he ends up drinking like a goy.)

His son related that every time his father, the holy Rebbi Shimon, would say a Dvar Torah at the third Shabbos meal, he would begin by saying, "Hashem created the world out of His desire to bestow goodness upon His creations." His son said that he heard Rebbi Shimon explain this as follows: The time of Minchah (the afternoon) on Shabbos is referred to as "a time of favor," because that time was the time right before the creation of the world (since the creation began on Saturday night, the first day of the week), when Hashem decided to create the world in order to make known His Kingship and His desire to bestow good.

The Final Years

As mentioned, Reb Shimon became blind in his latter years, yet his disability did not hamper his service of Hashem. Having committed much to memory, he could study without texts before him, and whatever he had not memorized he was not embarrassed to have read to him. He even continued traveling to Tzaddikim despite his blindness and likewise, as in his prime, received innumerable people in need of his wisdom and prayers.

Reb Shimon's wit remained sharp, and, although blind, he "saw" people quite clearly. When visiting Reb Shimon, it was customary to place a coin called a *"pertziger"* into a plate upon the table in front of the Rebbe, prior to beseeching the Rebbe's aid. Once, a certain unscrupulous person furtively removed a *pertziger* from the plate and then dropped the same coin back down before making his request. Reb Shimon then asked in Yiddish, *"Mit mir piter vilsdu mich shmiren?"* — "With my own butter you want to smear me?"

Reb Shimon stood very tall and broad, and in his old age his stomach became bloated. Given that he ate very little, people found the increasing size of his stomach perplexing. When asked about this phenomenon, he confided that his stomach grew with the troubles which befell the Jewish people. He added that even after his death and burial, his stomach would shrink and grow depending upon the condition of the Jewish people.

Reb Shimon considered one's life worth living only if it could be spent serving Hashem. For this reason, he always considered himself to be three years younger than his real age. The Belzer Rebbe, the Sar Shalom, once asked him how old he was, and when Reb Shimon gave his patented reply, the Belzer Rebbe indicated that he knew that Reb Shimon was older. Reb Shimon then confessed that "the days of my life are more than that by three years, but I do not take into account my first three years because during them I experienced no pains and, therefore, did not serve Hashem. Only those years spent in the service of Hashem do I consider as part of my life."

Like his cousin and primary teacher, the Chozeh of Lublin, Reb Shimon lived through the proscriptions of Vilna placed upon the Chassidic movement between the years 1780 and 1820 and strove to mainstream Chassidus, both from without by contending with its adversaries and from within by reforming those internal problems which helped fuel the opposition's fire. Many of the movement's new adherents were intoxicated with religious fervor, sometimes acting wildly in public by performing such antics as somersaulting, treating non-Chassidic rabbis with blatant disrespect and the like. Reb Shimon discouraged these acts and greatly helped to purify Chassidus of fanaticism. Also, in periods of intense poverty and ignorance, Reb Shimon's teachings were full of hope and inspiration for the common man. His *vortlach* emphasized the classic Chassidic philosophy that every mundane act could be elevated to the service of G-d with the proper intention. The poor farmer now had meaning in his life. G-d was now accessible to the unlettered and the vulnerable just as He was to the student and scholar, each according to his subjective, individual level.

Reb Shimon's life came to an end on the 15th of Tishrei in the year 5611 (1851). His soul departed on the first day of Sukkos while he held the Lulav and Esrog and performed the Mitzvah of the *Arba'as Ha'minim,* an appropriate culmination to a life completely immersed in Torah and Mitzvos. He was in his ninetieth year. He was buried in the cemetery of Farber-Pelkir, the resting place of many other Tzaddikim, including Rebbi Meir of Hosakov (the father of Rebbi Levi Yitzchak of Berdichev) and Rebbi Zecharya Mendel, the author of *Darchei Tzeddek.*

A large mausoleum was erected over Reb Shimon's grave, and the site became a place of prayer for many over the years. Unfortunately, it was destroyed during the Second World War, and the exact location of his resting place remained unknown — until very recently. As this book was being prepared for publication, Rav Doniel Rokeach, the Rav and Av Beis Din of the Yoruslav Beis Midrash (in Monsey and Boro Park), contacted me with the news that the family burial blot of Rebbi Shimon of Yoruslav had been located, and I had the merit and privilege of endowing the construction of a proper *ohel* over the gravesite. Restored as well is the opportunity for Jews to travel again to Reb Shimon, pray and gain inspiration and salvation in the merit of a Tzaddik.

Rebbi Naftali Maryles
of Litovisk

Rebbi Naftali Maryles, the Rebbe of Litovisk (Lutowiska), and a twin sister were born in 1828, when Reb Shimon was 67 years old. As babies, they cried incessantly, and Reb Shimon commented, *"Vos zai raisson zich, zai zennen fun alter"* — "it is no wonder that they are wild; they are children of my old age."

When Reb Naftali came of age, he was wed to the daughter of Rav Yissachar Berish, the son of Rebbi Shmuel Zunvil, the head of the Beis Din for the communities of Litovisk and Istrik, a disciple-colleague of the Chozeh of Lublin, and a good friend of Reb Shimon. Tragically, Reb Naftali's wife died during her first pregnancy, and Rav Berish offered him as a wife his granddaughter, the daughter of Rav Berish's son-in-law, Rav Yeshaya Zalman Kalish, who succeeded him as head of the Beis Din of Istrik.

Reb Naftali's primary Rebbe and mentor was his father. After Reb Shimon passed away, he studied under Rebbi Shalom of Belz, the Sar Shalom, a close friend of Reb Shimon.

With the Belzer Rebbe's death, Reb Naftali became a close disciple of Rebbi Yitzchak Isaac of Zidichev, who had also been close with Reb Shimon, and remained under his tutelage for seventeen years. It was, in fact, Rav Berish, Reb Naftali's father-in-law, who gave Reb Yitzchak Isaac his first *kvittel*. The families of Maryles and Zidichev have remained close for more than two hundred years until today and, G-d willing, will continue as such.

When the Zidichever Rebbe passed away, Reb Naftali was inconsolable at the loss of his mentor. The eulogy that he delivered was published in his book *Ayalah Shluchah*. Throughout these years of tutelage under great masters since the death of his father, Reb Naftali refused to succeed his father as Admor, a decision which was not well received by the Chassidim of the Yoruslaver Rebbe. Once, while he was visiting his father's grave, several of Reb Shimon's Chassidim locked the gate of the enclosed site and refused to release him until he accepted from them a *kvittel* and, in effect, the mantle of Admor. Reb Naftali relented but still refused to be called "Rebbe" and insisted instead upon the title *Moreh Hora'ah*. As such, he served as the head of the Beis Din of Litovisk and became renowned as a *talmid chacham* and *dayan* of distinction. He was one of the prestigious participants in the gathering of rabbinic leaders in Lvov in 1882.

Reb Naftali passed away on the eve of Rosh Chodesh Iyar in 1890. Some time passed with no replacement for him as Rav in Litovisk until his son, Rebbi Yaakov Koppel Maryles, took his place as Rebbe and Av Beis Din.

Reb Yaakov Koppel was born on the second day of Rosh Hashanah in 1852 and passed away on the second day of Rosh Hashanah in 1925. He emerged as an awesome Torah scholar and led his congregation in the ways of righteousness. He married Toiba Rachel, the daughter of the Av Beis Din of Sahl, Rebbi Yosi, who was the son of Rebbi Shmuel Zenvil (the son of Rebbi Yehudah Tzvi Brandwein from Strettin).

Rebbi Yaakov Koppel was succeeded by his son, Rebbi Avraham Moshe. (The rabbinate of Litovisk remained within the family for over one hundred years, until the community was destroyed in the Holocaust.) Rebbi Avraham Moshe's son, Binyamin Menachem, was born within the lifetime of his grandfather, Rebbi Naftali, and merited to hold Rebbi Naftali's hands at the time of his passing. Reb Binyamin Menachem moved to America and passed away on the second of Sivan in 1964 (5724). He was buried in Jerusalem. His son, Rabbi Yosef Maryles, inherited the writings of his grandfather Rebbi Naftali, and he published them under the name, *Ayalah Shluchah*, in New York in 1970. The Sefer is arranged according to the Parshiyos of the weekly Torah reading, Tefillah, and festivals. Woven throughout are *divrei Torah* from great Tzaddikim that cannot be found anywhere else, as well as a wealth of information about Rebbi Shimon of Yoruslav and the lives of his descendants from Litovisk. (Reb Yosef's grandfather, Rebbi Yaakov Koppel, the son of Rebbi Naftali, started the work of arranging his father's writings after his father's death. His grandson Reb Yosef merited to complete the project.)

One of Rebbi Yaakov Koppel's many children was Rivka Henya, who married Reb Chaim Noach, a holy and pious *shochet*. Reb Chaim Noach lived in the village of Piabusz (Podbuz) within the greater town of Drohobycz. They had many children, one of whom was my grandfather, Reb Shimon Maryles, named after his great-great-grandfather, the Yoruslaver Rebbe.

Reb Shimon Maryles, like his father, was a *shochet*, yet he followed in his father's footsteps not only professionally but spiritually as well, leading a tranquil life steeped in Torah and

Chassidus. It was his profound faith and unswerving trust in Hashem that enabled him to survive the unspeakable horrors that would soon engulf the Jewish people.

World War II, the Annihilation of European Jewry, and Rebuilding

Years of Tragedy and Indomitable Spirit

The rich tranquility of the centuries-old *shtetl* lifestyle in Eastern Europe would be shattered and completely obliterated when Adolf Hitler, *yemach shemo v'zichro*, rose to power in Germany in the 1930's. His state platform rested upon the premise that Germans constituted the master race while other peoples — and in his eyes, primarily the Jews — were inferior and worthy of destruction, and, in addition, that the shame of Germany's capitulation in 1918 would be avenged and her honor never again compromised.

On September 1, 1939, the arch-evil ruler of Germany initiated the German invasion of Poland, which, due to the famous Molotov-Ribbentrop Pact between Vyacheslav Molotov, the Soviet Foreign Minister, and Joachim von Ribbentrop, the German Foreign Minister, in August of 1939, brought under Germany's control the whole of Poland east of the Vistula River and gave Russia eastern Poland and Lithuania. Much of Eastern Galicia, including Drohobycz, was then within Russian territory.

Even during the two-year reprieve before Germany, in 1941, would violate its pact with Russia and invade eastern

Poland, tragedy struck Reb Shimon and his family. At the start of 1941, his twin daughters, Bluma and Roza (after whom my own twin daughters, Shoshana and Raizel, are named) contracted measles. Since it was a time of war, medicine was scarce, and the family's desperate attempts to obtain aid were to no avail. The sisters, aged just nine months, died. This was the first of many wartime calamities that befell the Maryles family.

On June 22, 1941, the Germans began their offensive to conquer Russia and again invaded Poland. By June 30, the first pogrom, in which over 200 Jews were murdered in Drohobycz, was carried out. This barbarity, of course, marked only the beginning of the total devastation and destruction of Drohobycz's Jewish community. Within the ensuing month, Jews were required to wear a yellow Star of David on the right sleeve, and all who failed to comply could be immediately shot. This marked the end of the Jews' basic human rights and the beginning of their systematic murder.

In August of 1942, the Germans and the Ukrainians carried out the first *aktion*, the gathering of Jews to be shipped to their deaths. They gathered Jews, young and old, men, women, and children, deporting thousands of Jews to the Belzec death camp, where they were gassed upon arrival. By October, Jews were required to relinquish their homes and property and be ghettoized. At that time, only 7,000 out of the town's 17,000 Jews remained. By the end of the war, all but 400 of the Jews of the district had been murdered.

In November, the second *aktion* began. Again perpetrated with the aid of the Ukrainians, it was barbaric in the extreme, with an aim at killing as many Jews as possible. By December, few Jews remained in the Drohobycz ghetto.

The members of the Maryles family who survived those

dark, doom-filled days owe their survival to my grandfather's brother, Reb Aharon, after whom I am named. I certainly would not be alive were it not for him, and to me it is a profound privilege to bear his name, and a responsibility that I only pray I can live up to.

As mentioned earlier, Reb Aharon was a genius who, with the powerful combination of his brilliance, his trait of love and kindness for his fellow Jew, and his bold resourcefulness, applied his genius in constructing bunkers which provided refuge for a large number of Jews. This master builder's first project was dug out beneath an apartment building in the Drohobycz ghetto and housed eighty members of his large extended family. The bunker was extremely elaborate, with running water, sewer drainage, a shower, a stove, and a year's supply of food. It also was equipped with an escape route leading into the city's sewer system. The family hid there while the Germans occupied the city and systematically began exterminating the city's Jewish occupants, until May of 1943.

Life — and Death — Underground

In the summer of 1942, Aharon's bunker was completed. The first *aktion* of August had not yet taken place, although it was imminent and tensions were high. The family decided that the time had come for them to enter the bunker.

Now, every parent surely knows that the ultimate form of *mesirus nefesh* is not surrendering one's own life but, rather, that of one's child. My grandfather, Reb Shimon, had a two year-old boy named Noach and feared that the child would make too much noise in the bunker. At that time, many Jews had placed their infant children in hospitals and orphanages, assuming that such institutions would not be subject to the privations and dangers of war, even at the hands of the Germans. For my Zayde to resort to separating from his son was an utter impossibility after having just buried his twin girls, little Bluma and Roza. However, it was equally impossible for him to selfishly bring Noach into the bunker and endanger the lives of all of the other occupants.

Characteristically, Reb Shimon rose to the test and pushed aside his personal needs and feelings, relinquishing his son to the care of a hospital. Later, a report reached him that the hospital to which he had entrusted Noach was not at all a safe asylum. The boy had been starved to death. The pain that my Zayde felt was indescribable in words. He carried it with him for his entire life, and that pain was a part of the grandfather whom I was privileged to know and love. Incredibly, however, he did not despair. He never abandoned hope, belief, and faith in Hashem but remained His steadfast servant and soldier, regardless of the circumstances and struggles that were his lot.

In April of 1943, the Drohobycz ghetto was liquidated, and the Germans systematically combed every building and destroyed every bunker they found where Jews were hiding. Aharon's bunker was so well-concealed beneath a particular apartment building that the Germans, although aware through hearsay of its existence, could not discover its exact location. They resorted to tossing grenades into the basements of the buildings in which they thought the bunker might be located. The suffocating smoke of the burning building drove all eighty members of Aharon's family out through the bunker's escape route and into the city's sewer system, where many were separated from the group and eventually caught and killed by the Germans or the Ukrainian police. Of their original number, only twenty remained, and of those killed were Reb Shimon's wife, Baila, and his mother, Rivka Henya (who was the daughter of the Litovisker Rebbe, Reb Yaakov Koppel, and for whom my daughter Rivka Henya is named). His son, Yehuda (or Yiddel, as he was affectionately called), was killed later by the Germans.

The survivors of the family regrouped deep in the forest near Pidbusz, a town approximately ten kilometers from Drohobycz where Reb Shimon and his father, Reb Chaim Noach, had lived before the war. Reb Shimon and his brothers had often traveled in the forest to buy furs from the forest ranger and knew the area well. Led by Aharon, with their extremely limited resources they began constructing a new, far more rudimentary bunker.

The group approached the forest ranger and his wife to buy food and supplies. The ranger was antagonistic, but his wife had pity on them and sold them grain, a shovel, and some utensils for cooking.

The new bunker was built mainly by hand. It had a stove, which vented through a tree trunk and was, thereby, well-camouflaged above ground. It had a toilet but was not equipped with water. Water had to be drawn and carried from a nearby creek at night so as to avoid contact with the Germans or the Ukrainians. The entrance to the bunker was concealed with twigs and grass, and with no connection to an electrical source, the interior was very dark.

These dismal conditions caused sickness and severe bouts of diarrhea for many members of the group, who were forced to bear the terrible stench of the accumulated waste. At one point during the winter, one of the more seriously afflicted members, who was not a member of the Maryles family, insisted upon relieving himself in the forest outside. The others of the group adamantly opposed this, fearing that his footprints upon the snow-blanketed ground would alert the Ukrainians to their presence. Despite their protests, this person left the bunker, and indeed, his footprints were noticed by some peasants, who alerted the authorities.

Ukrainian police soon surrounded the area of the bunker and began shooting. Aharon told Reb Shimon and his two sons, Yaakov (my father) and Berish (my uncle), as well as his other brother, Yoshe, to jump into the toilet pit. They and another person did so, and Aharon covered the pit with wood and twigs, concealing his two brothers and two nephews. Although his own wife and child were also with him in the bunker, he did not attempt to hide the child, who surely would have cried. Then he, his wife and child, and the rest of the group climbed out of the bunker and surrendered. Among this group was Reb Shimon's eldest son, Yehuda, who could not fit in the pit. In an effort to divert the police's attention away from the bunker and the toilet pit, Aharon began to run away from the area through the forest. The Jew-haters chased him and shot him. He knowingly and willfully sacrificed himself for the sake of saving others, and he died *al Kiddush Hashem*, in the sanctification of G-d's name, his pure and holy soul ascending to the highest of heights in the eternal world of truth. May his memory be blessed, may his blood be avenged, and may the merit of his righteous deeds protect us.

After running to the area of the bunker, the police descended into the bunker and removed all of the belongings, tools, and utensils. They traced the pots to the ranger's wife, dragged her screaming from her home, and shot her for aiding Jews. The ranger, who insisted that he had had nothing to do with his wife's insurrection, was left unharmed.

The whole of that day the police and various peasants kept returning to the bunker to marvel at its construction. Late at night, after many hours in the feces-filled pit, Reb Shimon, his two remaining sons, and his brother emerged and, without dry or clean clothing, made their way in the winter cold toward Drohobycz.

The tragic loss of Aharon occurred in December of 1943. Before his murder, he had disclosed to his brother the location of yet another bunker that he had built. This one was beneath the Schwartz family home at 59 Boryslawska Street in Drohobycz. As mentioned earlier, with the ghettoization of the Jews, the home and property were claimed by a Ukrainian named Ivan Bur, who, for an enormous price, agreed to allow the construction of the bunker beneath and adjacent to the basement. The impetus and organization of the entire project came from the Mayer family, who commissioned Aharon to build the bunker for them.

Moving only at night while hiding behind farmhouses and barns during the day, the small group painstakingly traversed the relatively short ten kilometers from the forest to Boryslawska Street in two days. The men arrived there freezing, soaked in sewerage and having just witnessed the savage executions of their last remaining family members. They had lost everything except their faith in Hashem.

Including the new arrivals, there were thirty-five people in the bunker which Reb Aharon had designed for sixteen. It was positioned within the earth, far below the floorboards of the front of the house, and in front of the cellar, which was under the rear of the house.

One entered the bunker through a small tunnel, angling down from the right rear corner of the basement cellar. It was sealed with a heavy cement slab which was covered by a layer of earth and straw blanketing the entire cellar floor.

In total, the bunker measured twelve meters (forty feet) in length and three meters (over six feet) in width. It was furnished with wooden bunk beds, a gas stove, a toilet, electricity, and air ducts joined to the sewer system. Water was stored in two large cisterns embedded in the earth beneath the beds.

The bunker's air, given that its source was through the sewer pipe, was quite stale. Also, the heat of the bunker was extremely oppressive, a circumstance that worsened as the number of people occupying the bunker increased. To offer a more tangible perspective, the bunker's living space could be proportionately likened to twelve people sleeping and living within a small bedroom, measuring ten by thirteen feet, equipped with bunk beds for four. That tight space would get even tighter as more people sought shelter.

The near discovery of the bunker described at the start of this book occurred just a few days after the Maryles family had entered the bunker. Shortly after the Germans had left the house, Ivan opened the cement hatch and informed them that earlier in the week a neighbor had seen the Maryles men and boys in the backyard, where they had huddled waiting for Ivan to come home, following their escape and two-day journey from the forest, and she notified the police that the Burs were hiding Jews. The Germans and Ukrainian police came, Ivan explained, and they dug around the house, penetrating deeply into the earth below the floorboards, and into the dirt beneath the cellar floor. After some hours, they left, exhausted and frustrated.

Aharon's ingenious precautionary buffer of earth at every exposable side of the bunker saved the life of every Jew in the bunker. This was just one of the many miracles which Hashem performed in those horrific times, saving the family from annihilation.

In April of 1944, Ivan brought ten more people into the bunker, to his own financial gain. To accommodate them, a third tier of beds had to be built atop the existing two-tier structure, narrowing the space between the top level and the ceiling such that it was impossible to sit up in bed.

Food was always a problem. My father, Reb Yaakov Koppel, has told me on many occasions that they lived on potatoes, potatoes, and more potatoes. Worse still, this diet, limited in variety and nutrition, was equally as limited in quantity. There was very little to eat, and people simply dreamed of no longer suffering hunger pangs. There were periods when water was also a problem. In the spring of 1944, there was a severe drought which caused a general famine and made the procurement of food even more challenging. In those days, Ivan brought even less food down into the bunker. By mid-April, the cisterns had dried up, and water had to be hauled down into the bunker by Ivan. Water usage had to be strictly limited to drinking. Sewerage, then, remained in the toilet, unflushed, for many days, and bathing was impossible. These factors contributed to a terrible, putrid stench which permeated the bunker's already stale air. Also, the drought coincided with the heat of spring and summer, so the bunker was excruciatingly hot. These combined conditions further oppressed the bunker's inhabitants.

There were many reasons why Ivan risked his life to hide Jews. In one sense, it afforded this young, adventurous gentile the opportunity to experience the thrill of defying the invading Nazis. In another, it imbued him with a sense of importance in the eyes of the people he was concealing, the only people who ever had considered Ivan to be important (and ever would). Primarily, however, he was inspired by money, which he received in abundance for his efforts.

Ivan's Plot

Originally, the Mayer family, which conceived of the plan to construct the bunker and engage Ivan in its upkeep, had brought a lot of money and other valuables into the bunker with which to barter with Ivan for food. The Mayer's close friends who joined them came similarly equipped. However, as time went on, the money dwindled. Also, Reb Shimon and his surviving family came with only the shirts on their backs. Ivan, therefore, found himself serving a group of Jews whose worth had been tapped, and he longed to turn things about in his favor.

By that time, a few Jews still remained in the ghetto, and some of those few had maintained stashes of gold and diamonds. This intrigued Ivan, and he determined to dispose of the original, now impoverished inhabitants of the bunker and replace them with fresh, paying Jews. He devised a plan of subjecting the inhabitants to a doctor's physical examination and having those whom the doctor deemed sickly injected with "booster" shots of poison. One of the young members of the group overheard Ivan confiding his plan to some of the latest inhabitants whose funds had not yet dwindled, and everyone was alerted to the danger.

The inhabitants held an emergency meeting and decided that their only salvation lie in improving everyone's appearance so that the doctor would not deem anyone expendable. In a frenzy, they set about washing themselves and their clothing with what little drinking water there was, combing and styling hair, trimming mustaches and beards, concealing illnesses, infections or injuries, and readying themselves to greet their possible executioner with a robust smile.

When the physician and Ivan descended into the bunker, they found everyone looking their best and seemingly happy and healthy. After his examination, the doctor refused to administer the shots, and Ivan's plan was foiled, but the inhabitants of the bunker now not only feared what might be lurking outside the house but, also, what was lurking upstairs.

Liberation and Recovery

Even with all of these problems, there existed a growing ray of hope. The Soviet offensive was dominating the German troops and was slowly retaking Russian territory, pushing the Germans back westward. Eventually, the Russians neared Drohobycz, while the group in the bunker monitored every report of the Russian advance on a radio that, early on in the war, they had managed to purchase on the black market through the agency of Ivan.

In the beginning of August of 1944, Ivan came down to the bunker and announced that the Russians would be in Drohobycz any day. That was the last that they saw of Ivan. Several days later, the group could not discern any noise coming from the house upstairs, as though it had been abandoned. Everyone soon understood that the Russians had arrived and that Ivan had fled. They also realized that they were now trapped inside the bunker with no one to lift the heavy cement slab concealing the opening from above. Reb Shimon suggested to the group that they could pry open the door by constructing a lever with some of the lumber used in making the beds. They dismantled some of the beds and made a lever, and with it they successfully moved the cement slab.

With trepidation, the group crawled up into the cellar and slowly ascended the stairs to the kitchen. The sunlight was blinding. This was the first time in nine months that my family had seen sunlight! Save for a few Russian soldiers, the street outside was deserted. Reb Shimon's brother, Yoshe, was so excited to see the soldiers that he ran outside and kissed them.

The soldiers told the group to walk down the block to an abandoned factory which had been taken over by the Russian army. When Reb Shimon, my father, and my uncles reached the shelter, they were able, for the first time in years, to begin focusing their energies upon the long process of mending their broken bodies, rather than on merely surviving. Physical recovery and healing was by no means an easy task. Their stomachs were swollen and distended from having lived on the verge of starvation for so long. Everyone in the family weighed under 100 pounds, and the form of their bones protruded through their skin. Gradually and through much effort, everyone regained much of his strength.

While Reb Shimon convalesced, the surviving Jews of the city of Krakow learned of his whereabouts and requested his services as a *shochet*. After recovering, he accepted the offer and traveled there, arriving in Krakow near the end of 1944, just before the winter.

Reb Shimon eventually perceived the need in his new city for a kosher establishment at which to eat, so he established a small restaurant in his home. Although he had enabled Krakow Jews to obtain kosher meat as well as kosher meals, Reb Shimon had achieved little solace in his difficult, broken world.

My father, Reb Yaakov Koppel, remained in Drohobycz over the winter, and both he and his uncle, Reb Yoshe, sold their belongings on the black market. Eventually, with neither material nor monetary worth, they went into business. Salt was processed in Drohobycz and was, therefore, an inexpensive commodity. In Lemberg it was not readily available and was more expensive, so my father and his uncle would purchase salt in Drohobycz and sell it for a profit in Lemberg. In Lemberg they would buy yeast and cigarettes at a low price and sell them for profit back in Drohobycz.

For his own part beyond the family business, Reb Yoshe joined the Drohobycz police force in order to aid them in capturing Nazi war criminals. Towards the summer of 1946 both he and Reb Yaakov decided to move to Krakow to be near their brother and father, Reb Shimon.

The cigarette black market was a huge business in Eastern Europe following the war. Poland was busy rebuilding itself, and as the production of cigarettes was not high on its list of priorities, its small domestic production could not satisfy the great public demand. Hungary, on the other hand, was producing vast supplies of cigarettes, but the problem was that it was illegal to ship them across the international border. This problem was circumvented by hiring Russian army personnel with legal traveling papers to go across the Polish border into Hungary, pick up a shipment of cigarettes waiting for them in the forest, and transport them back across the border into Poland. The "importer" would sell the cigarettes to middlemen who in turn would sell them to the general public.

When Reb Yaakov and Reb Yoshe moved to Krakow, they became middlemen in the cigarette trade. Eventually, Reb Yoshe wanted to become an importer and not just a middleman, and this entailed going into the Hungarian forest with the Russians and making a deal with the Hungarians. Reb Yoshe asked my father, Reb Yaakov, to accompany him, but

Reb Shimon forbade Reb Yaakov to go. Although it seemed like a superb business opportunity, my father's deference to and respect for his own father was too great to disregard his father's wish, and therefore he did not accompany his uncle. Tragically, the Torah's promise that one should honor one's father "so that your days will be lengthened" proved true, for Reb Yoshe was double-crossed, murdered, and left in the Hungarian forest. Yet another tragedy thus befell the family.

Immigration to America

$\mathbf{M}$y Zayde, Reb Shimon, eventually saw that the Jewish community of Poland was not being rebuilt; the destruction wrought by the evil Germans had so viciously consumed all but a fraction of Poland's three million Jews that the entire fabric of Jewish life and society was gone forever, irreparable. He saw that hatred of the Jews was so deeply ingrained and rampant in the psyche of Poles and other gentiles that it still reared its ugly head, even when most of the Jews had already been murdered. He conceded to the reality that he was now a stranger in what had been his family's home for hundreds of years.

He knew that Torah-observant Jews were emigrating to America, so Reb Shimon and my father sought visas to travel there. They were unable to obtain visas to travel directly to the United States, but they did get visas to Cuba, and they hoped to make it into America from there.

In the spring of 1946, the family went to Paris. From there, they were to travel to Cuba via New York. A few months later my father and uncle boarded a ship to New York, but Reb Shimon had to remain in Paris because his new wife had given birth to my uncle Herschel and was not allowed to travel out of the country with a child less than one month old. The ship docked in New York for two days before embarking to Cuba, and the Maryles brothers were met at the pier by Reb Shimon's brother-in-law, Reb Binny Mendel, and Reb Binny Mendel's son, David, who would become a famous cantor in New York and an active member of the Agudath Israel organization. Reb Binny Mendel had left Europe before the war and now used his connections to get visas for my father and his brother.

For the first time in many years my father had peace of mind to pursue his life in the free world. Freedom, however, presented its own dangers, for the temptations of living in the West as an "enlightened" Jew were then most enticing. Also, many survivors of the inferno of Europe were becoming avowed anti-religionists. Seeing his new freedom as an opportunity for growth and sensing the dangers of the American social climate of the time, my father assumed the "yoke of Torah" and enrolled himself in Yeshivas Torah Vadaas. He was not alone. There were other survivors who arrived upon American soil emotionally broken and with only the shirts on their backs, but who did not forsake the yoke of Torah in light of their impoverishment and pain but, instead, immediately began learning Torah, rebuilding the world that was lost.

Reb Shimon, meanwhile, was allowed to travel to Cuba from Paris via the United States. He arrived in New York with his new wife, Bella, and son in the winter of 1947. Reunited with his older sons, he stayed for just one month before being required by the immigration authority to travel on to Cuba, where he and his family lived for about six months.

Following the war, as before the war, the immigration policies of the United States were very strict. It is likely that the government feared admitting too many immigrants incapable of finding work and becoming a burden to society. Few of the

Jewish survivors of the inferno in Europe who sought entry into America were granted entry visas. There was, however, a shortage of qualified rabbis and *shochtim* in America, and when the Jewish community of Toledo, Ohio, heard that Reb Shimon was in Cuba, they petitioned the government to have him brought to their city as a rabbi and *shochet*.

The rabbinic authority in Toledo was Rav Katz, who was the brother-in-law of Rav Moshe Feinstein *zt'l*. Reb Shimon was granted permission to enter the country, and he settled into the Toledo community and served as the assistant rabbi and the *shochet* for sixteen years, until 1963. During that time, Reb Shimon found himself faced with another painful decision concerning his child.

Like most Jewish communities outside of New York, that of Toledo lacked a solid Torah educational infrastructure. Leaving Toledo for another city better suited for Jewish education was financially impossible, so my Zayde had no choice but to send his son to public school during the day and to a small *cheder* at night.

When my uncle was seven years-old, he came home from school humming a gentile holiday tune. Horrified, my Zayde phoned a contact in Detroit, Michigan, enrolled his son in the Jewish day school there, found a home in which he could board, and sent him off with no delay.

Although today it is commonplace for parents to send away their children to yeshivas and seminaries in other cities, this decision weighed heavily upon my Zayde. His memories of the loss of his wife and most of his children during the war were still raw. Indeed, the memory of the loss of his little son, Noach, whom he had sent away before the liquidation of the Drohobycz ghetto, to find refuge in a hospital where the boy was eventually starved to death, was still stinging his heart.

How could he now send yet another child, the solace of his life and the consolation of his pain, away from him? Also, being an immigrant in a new, strange country with little knowledge of English and of the society around him, was equally daunting. How could he send his boy, unprotected, into a world to which he himself was a stranger? He nonetheless rose above his fears with superhuman effort and sent his son to Detroit because he knew the importance of living as a Jew, which could only be accomplished through a Jewish education. Ensuring that his child learned Torah and developed into a G-d-fearing, Torah Jew was of far greater value to my Zayde than the tranquility that he otherwise would have enjoyed had he kept the boy at his side.

My father, Reb Yaakov Koppel, had remained in New York, where he learned in Yeshivas Torah Vadaas and studied *chazanus*, cantorial skills, on the side. Like his forebears, he believed in serving Hashem with all of the skills and talents that Hashem granted to him, and since Hashem had granted him a beautiful voice, he longed to become a professional cantor, to sing Hashem's praises and to inspire others. Unfortunately, the demand in America at that time for cantors was limited to the Conservative and Reform movements, so my father determined to set for himself a different professional goal.

My uncle Berish was drafted into the army during the Korean war in 1952, a time when the American armed forces were not as accommodating to religious soldiers as they are today. Saturday was a normal work day, and Jews were not excluded from their duties. My uncle refused to work on Shabbos and was brought before the commanding colonel, who wondered why only he, of all the Jews under his command, had a problem with working on Saturday. My uncle was adamant, however, and the colonel finally suggested that he be classified as a "Seventh Day Adventist," the only division which was exempt from working on Saturday. This division worked mainly in the army dental laboratory making teeth, and thus my uncle was re-assigned to that division, where he learned this profession well.

Back in the 1940's and early 1950's it was not easy to avoid working on Saturday. The official day of rest in America was then limited to Sunday, and only within the last few decades has Saturday also become a nationally recognized non-workday. Many Shabbos-observant Jews would take jobs on Monday only to find themselves the next Monday again looking for work. After completing the week, they would inform their employers on Friday that they could not work the next day and, invariably, would be told not to bother reporting to work on Monday as well.

My father took his first job as a cantor in Cincinnati at the synagogue of Rav Eliezer Silver, who, apart from being a great *talmid chacham*, is well remembered for his work with the Vaad Hatzala and his tireless rescue efforts on behalf of the Jews of Europe. This position was only for the High Holidays, so he sought other work as well. He soon decided to move to Chicago, where the Jewish community was larger, and where he could be closer to his father, Reb Shimon, in Toledo, Ohio.

Reb Yaakov Koppel took on many odd jobs in Chicago in order to avoid having to work on Shabbos. After some time, his brother also moved to Chicago. Together, they opened up their own business, calling it the "Maryles Dental Laboratory." Their primary purpose in opening their own business was to insure that they and their employees could earn a living without having to desecrate the Sabbath. They were in business for forty years until my father retired.

My Mother's Story

Reb Yaakov married my mother, Chana, in June of 1956. My mother's parents, Mordechai and Baila Laub, were born in Galicia, and they moved, after their marriage, to Mainz, Germany, a city on the Rhine River near Germany's western border. The Jewish community of Mainz was predominately Orthodox, and Reb Mordechai owned a couple of shops and lived a peaceful, pious existence.

When the accursed Adolf Hitler became chancellor of Germany in 1933, any peace enjoyed by the Jews was shattered. Immediately, Hitler began his assault upon the Jews, ordering a boycott against Jewish-owned business just three months after taking office. Following this, many top Jewish professors and doctors were dismissed from their universities and hospitals. Two years later, in September of 1935, the Nuremberg Laws were passed, and all civil rights of the Jews, including citizenship, were removed. Interestingly, this applied even to those Jews who had converted to Christianity and considered themselves avowed, practicing Christians.

These conditions within Germany prior to the outbreak of war caused many German Jews to emigrate, and between 1933 and 1938 approximately 200,000 Jews left the country. Unfortunately, many of those who emigrated lacked the foresight to place the Atlantic Ocean between themselves and Hitler, and they simply sought refuge by crossing the eastern border into Poland, where most of them were later murdered.

Germany sealed its own borders to Jewish emigration in 1938. The vast majority of the 225,000 Jews remaining in Germany would eventually be murdered.

Kristallnacht was the event that prompted Reb Mordechai to send his children out of the country. On the night of November 9 in 1938, Jews were attacked and synagogues were burned throughout the country. The windows of thousands of Jewish-owned shops were shattered, prompting the name *Kristallnacht*, "night of the broken glass."

The "night of the broken glass" was so horrific that most of the Western world, until that time aloof to Hitlerian propaganda and policies, was shocked. Hitler may have thought that he had gone too far too soon, so as though to appease the world he immediately established the "kindertransports" program in which 10,000 children were allowed to be sent out of Germany to England. Reb Mordechai immediately registered his six children for this program, and in December of 1938, the children boarded a train to Holland, from where they were to travel by boat across the English Channel to Great Britain. Obviously, this was a difficult measure for the parents to take. They knew that they may never see their children again. They nonetheless placed their faith in Hashem and entrusted their children into His hands.

By the time the Laub children reached Holland, the ships going to England were already full and were not accepting new passengers. The children were stranded in Holland without parents. To make matters worse, the Dutch government was extremely cautious about germs and diseases, so the children could not be brought into the interior of the country but, rather, were placed under quarantine in displaced-persons camps for six months.

Prior to the German invasion of Holland and the deportation and killing of Dutch Jews (in 1943), the Jewish community of Amsterdam opened its homes to Jewish refugees. My mother, Chana, was taken in by Yaakov and Rochel Baars, with whom she lived for about four years. During that period, her own parents, Mordechai and Baila, were murdered by the Germans, and she, just seven years-old, was an orphan in a strange land.

In May of 1940, the Germans invaded Holland and revoked the civil rights of the Jews. My mother continued attending the Jewish day school in Amsterdam, which remained open until the spring of 1943, when the deportations and killings began. She went into hiding that summer.

It is noteworthy that many gentiles in Amsterdam were commendable in their willingness to help and even hide Jews throughout the war. Leib Laub was about sixteen when he joined the Dutch partisan movement to fight the occupying Germans. Through his connections, he learned that the Germans were planning a massive round up and liquidation of Holland's Jews that spring. Desperate to spare his siblings this horror, he contacted the eldest of the Laub children, Esther, and told her to find people who could hide the family. Esther had a gentile teacher, Ms. Ovwelleen, with whom she was very close and confided in her. The woman was moved by Esther's dilemma and offered to arrange hiding places for all of the Laub children. Ms. Ovwelleen had a roommate, Ms. Hoefsmith, and together they arranged hiding places for over fifteen children as well as for some families.

Chana was sent to a small countryside village near the German border called America Limburg and was taken in by the Gverts family. The Gverts' were Catholics with seven children of their own and, like Ms. Ovwelleen and Ms. Hoefsmith, surely earned the distinction of righteous gentiles to have risked certain death for themselves and their large family by hiding Jews.

As she lived with her host family, Chana's "cover" was that she was a Catholic girl who had been living in Amsterdam, had fallen ill and, on the doctor's orders, had been sent to convalesce in the fresh air of the country. The Germans themselves were aware that Jewish children had been taken into hiding around the countryside, and they raided the villages often in search of such children. My mother, therefore, could not attend school, lest the school be raided, the identity of each child scrutinized, and she be discovered. To protect her during daytime raids on their own village, the Gverts family developed a signaling system by which Chana could be warned and could flee into the fields, where she would hide among the tall stalks until the danger had passed. When the Germans came at night, she was hidden underneath floorboards. My mother still remembers seeing the eyes of rats staring back at her in the pitch blackness.

To maintain her facade as a Catholic schoolgirl from Amsterdam, Chana had to attend church with the Gverts family. When I was a boy, my mother told me that she would recite the *Shema* while the congregation prayed. This act has always had a profound impact upon me. Chana was only a young child whose parents had perished. How easy, how natural, it would have been for her to embrace these new people and their traditions as her own. Would we, given the same circumstances, have resisted and clung so fiercely to a severed, obliterated past?

The English liberated America Limburg in the fall of 1944, and Chana remained in the region until May 5, 1945, the day on which Holland was declared completely liberated. She then returned to live with the Baars family and resumed her education and her still young, remarkably intact, Jewish life.

When she reached marriageable age, my mother felt that America would present more opportunities for marriage, and she moved to New York. Unaccustomed to so large a city, she eventually moved to Chicago, whose religious Jewish community was smaller than New York's but vibrant and promising in its own right. Indeed, soon after settling in, she was presented with an outstanding *shidduch* suggestion. Chana and Yaakov Koppel met and were married.

Reb Yaakov Koppel Maryles and Chana Laub were married in June of 1956. My uncle Berish also married shortly afterward. By 1963 both couples had been blessed with three children. The dental laboratory was getting larger, and my father and uncle were able to create a job for their father, Reb Shimon, enabling him to move to Chicago. My other uncle, Herschel, married in 1969. The sons of Reb Shimon brought twelve children into the world, who, in turn, would continue to rebuild the family by bearing children of their own and raising them in the path of their great forebears.

Zayde — The Final Years, Unceasing Growth

T oward the end of a lifetime filled with so much pain and suffering, my Zayde was able to reap the joy and fulfillment of living in the presence of his children and grandchildren. A Jew, however, must never stop growing, and my Zayde knew and lived this creed. Therefore, upon retiring from the family business, Reb Shimon and his wife Bella moved to Eretz Yisrael, to the city of Bnei Brak, in 1973, with his strong desire to immerse himself in that *heimeshe* environment of Yiddishkeit and Chassidus in which he had been raised and to which he had always longed to return.

Reb Shimon was by no standard a man of means, yet money was not important to him. He was more than thankful to be able to move to Eretz Yisrael and live on a meager, fixed income of a pensioner. When he decided to buy an apartment in Bnei Brak, there was talk of a Boyoner *shtiebl* being built there, and Reb Shimon was very excited about the possibility, as he had been very close with the former Boyoner Rebbe.

Those involved with the project sought to buy an apartment as the location for the shul but were short on funds, so Reb Shimon donated about five percent of the total purchase price of his own apartment. Put into perspective of today's market, his act equaled the donation of $12,500 (5% of $250,000) to a single institution, which was a great sacrifice for an older, retired individual living on a fixed income. However, Reb Shimon had always felt it extremely important to help rebuild what the Germans and their accomplices had destroyed, and being the man of action that he was, he put his money where his mouth was.

Like my father, Zayde was gifted with a beautiful voice, and he was a tremendously inspiring *ba'al tefillah*. In his new community in Bnei Brak, he davened from the *amud* during the *Yamim Noraim* in both the Sadgura (Sadigur) Yeshiva and the Boyoner *shtiebl*. People still tell me how exquisite and inspiring his *tefillos* were.

Reb Shimon always had a smile on his face. He was a living example of the Mishnah in Avos (1:15) that teaches that "one should always greet each person with a pleasant face." People who were depressed or downcast would feel much better after speaking with him; his warm cheerfulness, in spite of the incomprehensible suffering and challenges that he had faced in his lifetime, made everyone's problems seem trivial and insignificant. However, there was something else in him, something more subtle, from which people drew strength and solace. He had seen so many of his beloved family members vilely and ruthlessly dehumanized yet had retained his love of humanity and faith in G-d. Sensing that, when people spoke to him they were inspired to strengthen their own love and faith rather than hopelessly wither in fear and despair.

If a person believes that whatever befalls him in life is G-d's will, then he will be joyful, knowing that G-d wants only the best for each of us. This can be compared to a child who is ill who must take bitter medicine or undergo painful therapy or complicated surgery without understanding why he must suffer. Only when the child grows up and enjoys good health will he fully grasp that what he had earlier endured was actually saving his life. The same is true for all of us, who cannot understand the benefits of our suffering while we suffer and cannot see the truth — until only after we have died and entered the world of truth — of how our lives, our eternal lives, have been saved. Reb Shimon was never bitter, because he was able to maintain his faith that Hashem was administering medicine, the healing effects of which were unforeseeable to all except Him. Zayde knew that Hashem loved him, and Zayde lived his life accordingly.

Many people spend half a century working so that they might retire. And then what do they do? Absolutely nothing. Reb Shimon, however, regarded retirement as an opportunity to start working! In Bnei Brak, he would wake up at 4:00 AM and go for an hour's walk with his wife, Bella. Their predawn walk accomplished two things. It afforded them exercise and, also, time together, which truly made Bella happy, leaving her in that frame of mind for the entire day.

It is worth noting that many of us fail to do something *regularly* to make our spouses feel special; instead, we wait until a problem or an argument forces openings in our busy lives to show them our love. Of course, we then rise to the occasion, but, invariably, once the problems seem solved, those openings become sealed and then lost. Reb Shimon was not interested in such self-defeatism. He sought constant, positive progress, especially in his most important relationships, at all times. May we learn from his actions and not be shamed by them.

After the early-morning walk, he would go to shul to daven and then learn Torah. Before shul, however, he would have a cup of coffee to help give him strength. This was in accordance with the custom of his great-great-grandfather, Rebbi Shimon of Yoruslav, who recommended drinking something hot before davening in order to pray properly and emphatically. He would then return home for breakfast with his wife. After breakfast, he went back out to learn Torah until lunch. After lunch he would take a short nap and return to the Beis Medrash for Minchah and more learning. My Zayde would come home for dinner and then go out for Maariv and learn. Finally, he would come home and go to sleep. This is what Reb Shimon called retirement!

When Zayde reached his eighties, he began to fall ill. He underwent a few surgeries, but his war- torn and time-battered body steadily deteriorated. He died at the age of eighty-seven and was buried on Har HaMenuchos in Yerushalayim.

The teaching of the Tana, Rebbi Shimon, in Avos (4:13), inscribed upon the gravestone of my Zayde who bears his name, is most fitting: "There are three crowns: the crown of Torah, the crown of priesthood, and the crown of kingship, but the crown of a good name is greater than all."